# SKINHEADS,
# FUR TRADERS,
# AND DJS

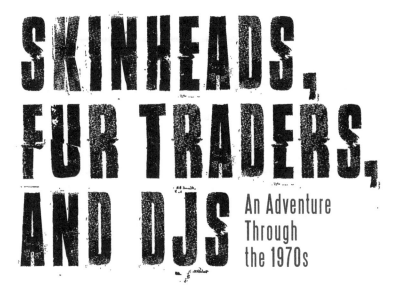

# SKINHEADS, FUR TRADERS, AND DJS

An Adventure Through the 1970s

## KIM CLARKE CHAMPNISS

DUNDURN

TORONTO

All images except when indicated are courtesy of the author.
Cover image: Courtesy of the author
Printer: Webcom

**Library and Archives Canada Cataloguing in Publication**

Champniss, Kim Clarke, 1954-, author
    Skinheads, fur traders, and DJs : an adventure through the 1970s / Kim Clarke Champniss.

Issued in print and electronic formats.
ISBN 978-1-4597-3923-9 (softcover).--ISBN 978-1-4597-3924-6 (PDF).--ISBN 978-1-4597-3925-3 (EPUB)

    1. Champniss, Kim Clarke, 1954-.  2. Disc jockeys--Canada--Biography.  3. Fur traders--Canada--Biography. 4. Hudson's Bay Company--Employees--Biography.  5. Video jockeys--Canada--Biography.  6. Television personalities--Canada--Biography.  I. Title.

ML429.C43A3 2017        781.64092        C2017-903402-2
                                          C2017-903403-0

1  2  3  4  5    21  20  19  18  17

Conseil des Arts  Canada Council    Canada    ONTARIO ARTS COUNCIL
du Canada         for the Arts                 CONSEIL DES ARTS DE L'ONTARIO
                                               an Ontario government agency
                                               un organisme du gouvernement de l'Ontario

We acknowledge the support of the **Canada Council for the Arts**, which last year invested $153 million to bring the arts to Canadians throughout the country, and the **Ontario Arts Council** for our publishing program. We also acknowledge the financial support of the **Government of Ontario**, through the **Ontario Book Publishing Tax Credit** and the **Ontario Media Development Corporation**, and the **Government of Canada**.

Nous remercions le **Conseil des arts du Canada** de son soutien. L'an dernier, le Conseil a investi 153 millions de dollars pour mettre de l'art dans la vie des Canadiennes et des Canadiens de tout le pays.

VISIT US AT

dundurn.com | @dundurnpress | dundurnpress | dundurnpress

Dundurn
3 Church Street, Suite 500
Toronto, Ontario, Canada
M5E 1M2

*For Cameron and Eliot …*

# CONTENTS

# CHAPTER 1

# London

"That bloke's screwing me. There's gonna be bovver," said Mick, with a worried voice. It was Saturday night at the Hammersmith Palais, one of the premier discos in London, a huge old ballroom that attracted the toughest lads and the cutest girls. Mick was shouting over the DJ's music, ironically, "Love Train" by the O'Jays. I wasn't paying attention, as I was standing by the music booth watching the DJ skilfully cue the next single on the turntable, hoping I might learn something. This was 1972 — a period in the United Kingdom when "screwing" meant someone was staring you down. The "screw" usually happened just before the bovver boy walked over and cracked you with a Glasgow kiss. With the victim on the floor, Jack the Lad would then stick the boot in, usually Doc Martens, aiming for the goolies, leaving the victim writhing in agony with his future fatherhood in question. No Love Train for these hooligans.

I knew what was coming next. It wasn't that Mick had done anything wrong, in particular; it was just that the bloke in question wanted to fight. This was an era of recreational violence. It was *A Clockwork Orange* for real. As fun-loving eighteen-year-olds, we were used to trouble. Not that we ever went looking for it, but on our tours around the discotheques of southwest England in search of the best nightclubs, we would usually be involved in a fight, witness one, or be running away from one. It just went with the action. And if you were walking home at night, you had to stay clear of certain street corners where the skinhead gangs congregated, particularly outside fish and chip shops; or if you caught the last bus home, you didn't sit on the upper deck of the red Routemasters but found a seat downstairs close to the conductor, who offered a hint of security.

Mick was always getting into trouble. He used to say he had all the bad luck and I had all the good luck. I used to tell him you made your own luck. But bad luck was true of Mick. Maybe it was his confidence or sly smile; whatever the reason, bad luck always seemed to dog him. He would pull some bird, and then the next minute some unknown bloke would jump him. So we left the Palais, its soul music and its packed dance floor, and hurried out into the cold December night air of Hammersmith Broadway, thankful we had given Trouble the slip.

As we were walking up to the heart of the Broadway, one of the busiest intersections in all of London, with a multitude of roads all converging in one central area, and a hub for the London tube, a half a dozen guys turned the corner, headed toward us. They were older, in their mid-twenties, and looked like dockers from the east end. We braced ourselves for certain trouble, so we kept our heads down, hoping to avoid eye contact. But as they drew near, we could see they had already been in a fight. Two of them had blood running down their faces. They were holding their heads, trying to ease the pain, and it looked like one had been stabbed. They walked right by us. "Wow. I wonder who did that," I said. We soon found out.

As we rounded the corner, there was a gang of black lads about six to eight strong. They were bragging to each other with thick Jamaican accents about the fight. Two of them were holding steel rat tail combs, with the sharp ends deliberately pointed out like switchblades. These combs were popular among some skinheads at the time. They could plead innocence if the cops stopped and searched them for weapons. Unfortunately, this time we made eye contact. They took one look at us and sensed our fear. The chase was on. We ran for our lives — literally.

Hammersmith Broadway has a labyrinth of pedestrian underpasses. Not only do they allow people to get to the other side of the street by going under the continually busy roads, but they also link with the various entrances to the London Underground subway system. Mick and I dashed down the steps of one of these tunnels to make our escape. But when we got to the end, the gang was charging down the stairs to meet us head-on, shouting obscenities: "Get the fuckers!" They had jumped over the roadside railings and dodged through the busy traffic in an attempt to cut us off. Frightened, we immediately doubled back as fast as we could and took another tunnel, and then another one, and then another one.

Now this wasn't the first time I had been chased around Hammersmith Broadway. The football team I supported, Fulham FC, was just a mile or so away, so on game days, having caught the 267 bus to the Broadway, I would walk to and from the ground along Fulham Palace Road, proudly wearing my black-and-white club scarf. The problem was that there were also two other football grounds close by: Chelsea and Queens Park Rangers. Sometimes after a game, the warring factions of supporters — the Shed from Chelsea and the Loftus Road Boys from QPR — would meet at Hammersmith and there would be a rumble. And it wouldn't be just large packs causing trouble. Groups of threes and fours would pick on a lone supporter of the opposing team and steal his football scarf as a trophy. The leader would then knot the scarf in the belt loop of his Levi's jeans and let it dangle like a scalp claimed in a Wild West massacre. It was not unusual to see individuals with three or four scarves of various colours hanging from their waists, proudly claiming how hard they were as they strutted down the street in their Doc Martens and turned-up Levi's.

Knowing the various entrances to Hammersmith tube station allowed Mick and me to dodge the gang and make it back to my dad's Triumph 2000 that we had borrowed for the night. We were scared and out of breath, our hearts beating fast, but we were safe. We quickly drove off, full of false bravado, talking excitedly about how we had managed, once again, to give Trouble the slip.

We headed to our base of operations, and relative safety, the Bird's Nest in Twickenham. This is where I had originally met Mick. Two teenagers, both under legal age, who, in their love for music and night-life, had ventured into this local discotheque of dubious reputation by themselves. We had met at the bar, both visibly young, both visibly out of our depth in this "adult" club, and both on our own. We became a team. Within a year, we had become not only legal but also known to all the other regulars in the club. We could drink, dance, meet girls, expand our group of friends, and revel in the delight of walking into the club and having the bouncers, the bartenders, and the DJs know us by name. It was teenage heaven. On one particular night, Mick had lost his stylish tam-o'-shanter cap while dancing. The DJ, with whom we had become friends, particularly me, as I hung out in his booth trying to learn his skills, took to the microphone and, over the James Brown tune "Sex Machine," had the crowd chanting, "Where's Mick's hat? Where's Mick's hat?" It was *Saturday Night Fever* five years before that movie became a cultural reference point. That night after our scare at the Palais, we danced and flirted with the girls and forgot about our daytime realities.

## CHAPTER 2

# Damned Young

I came on the scene the same year as rock 'n' roll: 1954. "Shake, Rattle, and Roll" by Big Joe Turner made number one, the genre's first chart-topping hit, Elvis recorded "That's All Right (Mama)" at Sun Studio in Memphis, and Bill Haley and His Comets released "Rock Around the Clock." Originally released as a B-side, the song became a worldwide teenage anthem; when, the following year, it was used as the theme song for the motion picture *Blackboard Jungle*, the song and the genre were propelled into the mainstream. The movie was banned in some U.K. cinemas because fights broke out amongst rival teenagers. This "devil's music" had that kind of effect on young people. But I was born a long way from that entire hullabaloo.

My birthplace was Manama, Bahrain, in the Persian Gulf. Even today few people have heard of the country (except when news outlets mention its modern U.S. naval base or factor it in with trouble in the Middle East), let alone in the mid-fifties. It was then part of the British Commonwealth, strategically important, rich in oil, and a crucial stopover for British planes on their way to Australia and the Far East. My father, an Englishman, was the aerodrome commander. My mother, an American and a former journalist with the *Baltimore Sun* and the *Montreal Gazette*, taught English to Arab girls at the American School. It was the Arab girls who gave me my name before I was even born. They would point to my mom's pregnant belly and say "*Yemken*" meaning "perhaps" or "maybe." My mother, who loved nicknames, took that as inspiration, and I became "Kim." The family moved back to England in 1956 (the year of the Suez Crisis), and then luck played a big part in my involvement with pop culture. But it wasn't a musical moment; it was a visual one. My parents had enrolled me and two of my brothers in acting classes, and that led to small roles in commercials and a few movies. One part in particular would follow me for the rest of my life. I was a child of the damned.

One of the most recognizable shorthand images in pop culture for alien beings is the extraterrestrial children from the 1960s MGM horror movie *Village of the Damned*. The image of young people with eyes that light up, and with the power to control mere mortals, has become an archetype in both rock 'n' roll and movies. And here's what's wonderfully weird: I was that original child; I played the parts of both the boy and the girl when those frightening eyes illuminate for the first time in the movie. The producers just changed the wig and the clothes so that I could play both gender roles. Hey, I was in drag years before Boy George! It's not as if I had a major role. I didn't even have a speaking part. But it's a pivotal moment in the movie. The film sequence in which I was involved lasts just one minute and fifty-eight seconds, but it would have a profound impact on movie history and pop culture.

The modest-budget flick (just eighty thousand pounds), with legendary actor George Sanders in the lead role, gained positive reviews and, over the years, a cult following. The glowing eyes of the blond-haired children became iconic. That image not only continued through a long line of horror movies but was also appropriated by rock 'n' roll; for example, on David Bowie's *Heathen* album cover and in Michael Jackson's "Thriller" video. As if, by being literally in tune with this unnamed source of energy, one exists on a different plane. And that small part, that small piece of trivia, has followed me my whole life. I'll go to my grave with the inscription on my tombstone: a child of the damned.

My parents encouraged my acting until I was nine years old (I was signed to an exclusive contract for a year to be the Quaker Oats boy when I was six), and then something else dominated my formative years — music. Music emanated from almost every room in our big, old house. My three older brothers each had a record player in their bedroom and extensive record collections. My oldest brother hung around the Crawdaddy Club in Richmond, whose house band was a young local group — the Rolling Stones — and later, the Yardbirds. My parents had the radio switched on constantly in the breakfast room. Some of my earliest memories are tied to music. In the early sixties I would fall asleep listening to pop music played on Radio Luxembourg, which broadcast in English at 7:00 p.m. every night and played pop music till the early hours. I remember watching Elvis performing "Can't Help Falling in Love" on a clip aired by the BBC and being captivated. My brothers taught me how to do the twist to Pat Boone's "Speedy Gonzales" and persuaded me to perform my party piece whenever they brought girlfriends home. While I was still young, they would get me to stand by the portable record player and "DJ" at their parties by pressing the eject button to allow the next single, stacked on the turntable spindle, to drop down quickly after the previous song finished to keep the music going. In the solitude of my bedroom, I would stand in front of the mirror holding my tennis racket as if it was a Fender guitar, pretending I was Hank Marvin of the Shadows, and "playing" along to the classic instrumental song "Apache."

When I was nine years of age, I used my birthday money to buy my very first records: "Come On" by the Rolling Stones and "I Get Around" by the Beach Boys. That year of 1963, my mother, who worked for the neighbourhood newspaper, interviewed the Rolling Stones, who had graduated from the local club circuit and now made their first appearance on *Thank Your Lucky Stars*, a pop program that was shot at the local Teddington Studios. The following year, she had interviewed Paul McCartney from the Beatles and actor Wilfrid Brambell (who played Paul's dad) for the movie *A Hard Day's Night*, which was being staged at nearby Twickenham Studios. The TV show *Ready Steady Go!* became my window through which I could see what was going on in the pop world.

Around this time I was given a transistor radio, a revolutionary piece of technology in the early sixties, and I walked around with the device seemingly co-joined to my ear. The gift coincided with the birth of pirate radio, and Radio London and Radio Caroline became huge parts of my world. So much so that in 1967 I entered a contest for ITV's children's show *Five O'clock Club*, hosted by Muriel Young (who would later produce shows featuring the Bay City Rollers and Marc Bolan). The contest required viewers to write on the back of a post-card, describing their dream job for a day. I sent in an entry express-ing my hope of working for Radio Caroline. A week or so later, I was thrilled to receive a phone call from one of the producers. I hadn't won the contest, but they were producing a teenager's talk show in which young people could question and put forward their views on pirate radio to a government representative who was instrumental in closing down the illegal offshore stations. The government wanted to sink the pirates! Of course I wanted to be there. I was only twelve years of age, so my mom had to accompany me to the studio. I found myself on TV, with older kids, talking about how important I thought twenty-four-hour pop music was in young people's lives. Years later, I was amazed to discover a strong Canadian connection to British pirate radio. Canadian Keith Hampshire (later to have a string of hits of his own) had been a DJ, and some Brit-born jocks also had connections: Dave Cash had lived and worked in Vancouver for CFUN, and Tom Lodge, who was music programmer and DJ for Radio Caroline, had worked for the CBC before going on the air with the "pirates." Lodge would return to Canada in the 1970s and establish the Music Industry Arts program at Fanshawe College in Ontario. Allan Slaight, later to be the founder of the Canadian radio network Slaight Communications, worked in Radio Caroline's sales department and was responsible for the highly successful promotion "Cash Casino." By a wonderful karmic coincidence, many years later I would be hired to produce and write the tribute to the inductees for the Allan Slaight Honour at *Canada's Walk of Fame.*

By the time I was fourteen my musical tastes had finally become honed, as had my knowledge of Britain's many teenage tribes. My overriding passion for one style of music, roots rockabilly, gained me entry into the worlds of the "rockers" — greasers who idolized the leather-jacketed motorbike set — and the "Teddy Boys" — a teenage subculture that had died off in the late fifties but was then making a small comeback. It was my love of songs and artists from that era, especially Buddy Holly, that began to define me. I collected everything that Buddy Holly had ever recorded, searching out obscure releases in second-hand stores in the backs of shopping arcades. And it wasn't just Buddy, but early Elvis, Chuck Berry, Johnny Burnette, Duane Eddy, Eddie Cochran, and Gene Vincent. I had become hooked on that roots rock sound through my eldest brother's extensive record collection. I even "borrowed" his rare poster of Gene Vincent and pinned the "Be-Bop-a-Lula" star above my bed. Vincent, like Buddy, had been dead for a number of years. Even that myth fascinated me, an artist dying for the music. I didn't limit myself to just that 1950s musical era, as I still purchased the hits of the day and listened to my brothers' soul collections, especially Tamla Motown. But it was that frenzied early sound of rock that I adored. I was out of musical step with the vast majority of young people, but that gave me an identity. I began to search out the fashion of that fifties era as well, buying pointed-toe winkle-picker boots and fancy buckled belts to adorn my straight leg trousers. At my school, Latymer Upper, I was able to incorporate these elements into my uniform, much to the chagrin of my teachers. And as I walked down the school corridor, the whispers from the other students, who owed allegiance to other teenage subcultures, such as skinheads, mods, hippies, or just regular hardworking academics, would occur. My classmates teased me with the nickname "Greased Lightning" (I was also a fast runner on the school athletic team and a speedy winger on the football team). It was my first lesson in rock 'n' roll. You are the image you create.

When I turned sixteen, I completed the rocker image by purchasing a second-hand, on-its-last-tires 1959 Norton Jubilee motorbike for twenty pounds. It was a tank of a bike, with extensive side panelling, but I stripped it down and it looked pretty cool. However, it was always breaking down (no wonder, for twenty pounds!). It was forever in pieces in the garage, and at one time even in the breakfast room (something my siblings have never let me forget, even to this day). My father hated it. As he did my studded leather jacket and greased-back hair.

Me, aged sixteen, during my rocker phase.

"What will the neighbours think?" he asked me. As if I cared. But, boy, I thought I looked cool. That bike didn't last long, so I upped the ante and purchased a 1960 BSA C15 for forty pounds. It was a more-reliable, lightweight 250 cc bike, and it allowed me to motor to and from school and, more important, connect with a group of fellow-minded bikers in Wembley in North London, one of whom went to Latymer and was a mechanical genius. There was nothing more thrilling at sixteen years of age than being in a pack of motorcycle riders racing down the highway.

The shops that sold traditional Teddy Boy and rocker gear were rare. But one store on the fashionable King's Road in Chelsea gained a reputation as a one-stop boutique where you could not only buy drape jackets, bootlace ties, and thick-soled "brothel creeper" shoes but also hang out and listen to a jukebox programmed with fifties tunes. I would ride my BSA up there and walk around the store, looking at all the gear and listening to the classic tunes. The shop was originally called Let It Rock and later changed to Too Fast to Live, Too Young to Die. The owner encouraged his youthful customers and their purchases. That man was Malcolm McLaren, later to gain notoriety as manager of the Sex Pistols.

Of course, I had to be wary of skinheads, the sworn rival of every rocker, especially because my love of football took me into their world and strongholds: the hooligan ends of the soccer stadiums. There were two competitions during game day. There was the contest on the pitch, and the other concerned the hard core fans. Every ground had a certain section where the toughest supporters congregated and where the singing and chanting originated. It had its own name; for example, the Shed at Chelsea, the Kop at Liverpool, and the Stretford End at Manchester United. In those days, three-quarters of the grounds were terraces (standing only) and you could move around the stadium with relative ease. The hooligan fans from the visiting team, if they considered themselves tough enough, would attempt to take over that area where the opposition firms gathered — similar to the game of "capture the flag," except real pain was inflicted — or home fans stormed the area where away fans were standing. You had to be wary of displaying your team's colours — and for me doubly so, because I had to make sure I did not reveal elements of my greaser lifestyle. So on Saturdays when I ventured to Fulham to see my football team and stand among the skinheads of the cheering section at the Hammersmith End, I had to make sure I showed no trace of my rocker allegiance. One telltale sign, and I would have gotten my head kicked in by either fellow Fulham supporters or those of the opposing team. One day, I inadvertently wore my winkle-picker boots to the game. No one noticed, as we were crammed together on the terraces, but as I was walking toward Hammersmith on the way home, two skinheads pointed at my footwear, laughed, and began to intimidate me by following close behind. I thought I might not make it to the tube station in one piece. However, they lost interest and let me go my own way.

There had been a rockabilly revival in the U.K. in the early 1970s. Guitar whiz Dave Edmunds covered Smiley Lewis's 1955 song "I Hear You Knockin." It hit number one in the U.K. Christmas 1970. Creedence Clearwater Revival had a top ten hit with the 1950s flavoured "Travelin' Band." And there was a purist rockabilly revival group called the Wild Angels who had a cult hit with the album *Live at the Revolution*. The cover featured the Brylcreemed band members with their DA (duck's ass) haircuts, standing astride their motorbikes looking menacing. It was a must for any rockabilly fan. Needless to say, all those records were part of my collection. On the back of that wave of popularity, a massive rock 'n' roll revival show was staged at the famous Wembley Stadium in the summer of 1972. It featured the greatest names of the genre: Bill Haley and His Comets, Chuck Berry, Bo Diddley, Jerry Lee Lewis, and Little Richard, among others. It was the first ever rock concert at the storied venue. Over sixty thousand rockers, greasers, and Teddy Boys attended the event. I, along with my small band of biker friends from Wembley, was there. It was a coming together of the rockabilly tribes, and as it turns out, it was a musical peak for many of the aging stars. There were also hundreds of skinheads outside the venue, looking to cause trouble with their arch-enemies. Something historical also happened, which at the time was perceived as ridiculous and totally out of place with the legendary musical lineup. The Detroit band MC5 also performed. Not only were they unknown by the roots rock crowd, but they also appeared to be making fun of the music. Lead singer Rob Tyner wore a gold lamé suit and exaggerated pointed-toe boots. They appeared to be a caricature of the culture, and the crowd booed and bottled them. They cut short their set for their own safety. The MC5 would later be cited as the prototypical punk rockers, and music purists would consider any fan lucky to have witnessed any of their outrageous performances. Not so on that particular day at Wembley Stadium. As it turns out, Malcolm McLaren was also there that day as well, selling T-shirts from his Let It Rock boutique.

After the concert my friends and I were invited to a house party nearby. We rode our bikes there, about a dozen of us roaring through the streets pumped up from the show. The party was held in a flat on the top floor of a house. It was packed with greaser chicks, leather-jacketed blokes, and one Hells Angel wearing full colours. (The first official chapter of the U.K. Hells Angels had been recognized by the California originators in 1969.) One of the bikers had left to purchase beer, and he was late in returning. His girlfriend, concerned, had kept an eye out for him by leaning out of an open window. Suddenly she shouted out, "Al's in trouble!" Apparently his bike had broken down a hundred yards from the party, and a group of about thirty skinheads had surrounded him and were threatening bovver. Once the word went up, the party emptied in a hurry and about twenty leather-clad rockers, jackets adorned with studs, chains, and various insignias, went charging down the street. My friends and I, not wanting to be left out of the rumble, joined the troop. We weren't too sure what we were going to do; we weren't fighters. But you don't think about that when you are in the middle of a frenzied moment. You just join the rabble.

We all stormed down the staircase and spilled out into the dark street. Heavy motorcycle boots crashing down on the concrete pavement signalled our imminent arrival. It must have sounded like Hannibal's army coming over the mountains. The individual leading the charge was our Hells Angels associate — someone we didn't know but were glad to have on our side. Most of the skinhead gang ran when they saw us coming. But their leader, a tough-looking guy with a number one crop, Doc Marten boots, bleached Levi's, and braces, stood his ground, which was unfortunate for him, as he had to tangle with the Hells Angel. The bloke didn't last long, and turned and walked away after taking a bad beating. Luckily nothing too serious happened, but it turned out to be my last foray into the world of bikers and roots rockabilly.

One night, soon after that skirmish, I was returning home from Wembley on my BSA. It had rained that day, so I wore my screaming-yellow crash helmet, not for safety but to keep my long wet hair out of my eyes. I rarely wore the helmet, as they were not compulsory in the U.K. until 1973. I travelled up one side of Harrow Hill, my lightweight bike chugging its way up the steep incline, through the rain and the darkness. I reached the peak and made my way down the other side. The bike picked up speed, and before I knew it I was travelling at over fifty miles an hour. I throttled back and applied the brakes as gently as I could, but the C15 began to hydroplane and slipped out from under me, eventually going one way and me the other. I somersaulted down the road into the inside lane and ended up in the gutter. Thank goodness there weren't any cars on the road at that moment. I was bruised, my skin scraped beneath my jeans, but nothing was broken except my winkle-picker boots. Luckily, the helmet had saved my head from serious damage. My bike had slid further on down the road. It, too, was bashed up, the handlebar crooked and the foot brake pedal bent, but still in working order, so I drove home carefully. The accident did not affect my love of riding bikes, but my teenage world took a seismic shift shortly thereafter for another reason altogether.

A Canadian friend of my brother Waynne (who had immigrated to Nova Scotia a few years earlier) was visiting England and staying at our house. My two remaining brothers wanted to show him some of the local entertainment and arranged for a night out at a nearby discotheque, Cheekee Pete's, housed in the Castle Ballroom in Richmond. The Castle had been a big mod hangout in the mid-sixties, and later became a skinhead stronghold. The local newspaper, the *Richmond and Twickenham Times*, often reported on battles that took place outside the venue. By the early seventies things had calmed down, but it still had a notorious reputation. For the first time ever my brothers invited me to accompany them, even though I was underage. They also told me to make sure I wore no traces of my rocker allegiance. As we entered the building to pay the entrance fee, I lit a cigarette in the hope that it made me look older. My brothers and our Canadian guest kept me in the middle of the huddle to hide me as much as possible. The bouncers on the door looked like they once worked for the Kray twins, even though they were outfitted in smart dinner jackets and bow ties. Their white shirts gleamed bright under the black lights of the entranceway. We made it into the discotheque without any grief. And there I was, surrounded by the music, the lights, the girls, and the excitement of a real club! The music grabbed my soul and didn't let go: songs such as "Tired of Being Alone" by Al Green, Wilson Pickett's "Funky Broadway," lots of Motown that included the Jackson Five's "ABC" and Edwin Starr's "War," slow tunes such as "Hey There Lonely Girl" by Eddie Holman, and the music of the skinheads — "Israelites" by Desmond Dekker and "Double Barrel" by Dave and Ansell Collins. I remained unobtrusive in the corner all night but watched, listened, and loved what I saw and heard.

My life changed dramatically after that. I traded in my leather jacket for a fashionable jacket and my winkle-picker boots for platform shoes, and my long hair was cut and styled at the local unisex salon. With no friends who had yet gained entry into this magical world of entertainment, I began to visit Cheekee Pete's on my own. I'd keep my head down, a cigarette in my mouth, and memorize a fictitious date of birth in case the bouncers asked me my age. In those days, the little red book that was the U.K. driver's licence didn't have a holder's photograph or a date of birth (it was considered an invasion of one's privacy!). All I had to do if the bouncers stopped me was sound convincing. Once inside I would make one pint of beer last all night (being still a schoolboy, I had limited funds), but I would dance the night away. It was part of the culture that guys and gals could take to the floor by themselves and just dance. Going solo on the dance floor was totally acceptable. This is what gave me validity. Possibly, it was my acting background that gave me the confidence for such audacious behaviour. I danced unabashedly, incorporating the mod moves I had learned from my brothers into my rocker moves. Something magical happens when you become unselfconscious, just dancing away. I would be there early (the chances of gaining entry into the club were always better in the early evening), and take to the floor before it got crowded. It would be the spark that encouraged other people at the club to get up and dance. The DJs loved that, and I became part of the community. Soon, some of my school friends wanted to join me at the disco, and it was the start of my fascination and commitment to the world of nightlife.

One night my classmate Barry and I planned a night out at Cheekee Pete's. He lived in Wandsworth, too far to travel home that late at night, so he arranged to spend the night at my house. I met him in the early evening at Richmond Station, the gathering spot for so many people even today, as it's the last stop on the Underground District line if you are heading out to the southwest London suburbs. The distance from the station to the disco was just a five-minute walk through the busy shopping area. We both managed to gain entrance to the club without any hassle and stayed till closing time. Skirting the drunken and boisterous groups that forever hang around outside a club when the action dies down, we made our way home. The last bus back to Hampton Hill was long gone, so we had to walk the dark route over Richmond Bridge and through Twickenham, where the road branched off toward Teddington on the left and Hampton on the right. It would take us about an hour. As we crossed the bridge that spanned the Thames, we heard the sound of footsteps racing to catch up with us. We both looked behind just to make sure we were not going to be jumped. It was a skinhead, not overly tall, but barrel-chested and wearing a heavy navy-blue Crombie coat with a pocket handkerchief proudly poking above the breast pocket. He asked us if we were heading toward Teddington. We told him we were going halfway there. "Can I tag along?" he asked. "Three of us together is good for protection." We agreed, and so he joined us on our walk. We introduced ourselves. His name was Freddie and he, too, had been at the Castle Ballroom. We got the sense that somebody was looking for him that night to do harm. After a long walk making small talk, we passed the Bird's Nest in Twickenham and Freddie asked if we ever frequented the club. I told him that I had recently started going. "I might see you there," he said. When we reached the junction where the road split we said our goodbyes. There was no trouble along the way, and we had enjoyed his company. Later on, when I described our acquaintance to friends, I found out Freddie was a notorious hard nut who had a bad reputation in the area. I thought that chance meeting might help later on. It didn't.

The Bird's Nest in Twickenham had opened in February 1968, with former Radio Caroline DJ Simon Dee manning the turntables. It was the first of a string of discotheques opened by Watney's brewing company. It was located just a hundred yards from the pedestrian bridge across the Thames that connected with Eel Pie Island, the home of a famous hippie hangout. When it had first opened, it gained attention for a simple gimmick — there were telephones in each booth that allowed occupants to order food and drink. It had a fairground decor and a stainless steel dance floor. By the time I started going to the club the phones were broken, but the dance floor was always packed. It was at the Bird's Nest that I met Mick at the bar. We became an instant partnership. And with the use of my dad's Triumph 2000, we were able to venture further afield in our pursuit of good times. We were out almost every single night. Discotheques became central to our lives. Friday nights, two or three cars would pull up outside my parents' house as our social group got bigger. And if I wasn't partnering Mick and the boys in some adventure to find the next undiscovered disco, I was dating a girl I had met at one of the clubs. It was almost as if we were making up for lost time, or trying to pack in as many urban adventures as was possible, not realizing that I would soon leave England and those carefree years.

# CHAPTER 3

# The Discotheque

People have tripped the light fantastic to records ever since the early days of the phonograph, most particularly during the 1920s Jazz Age and into the 1930s. In the 1940s the jukebox became the instrument that would act as a catalyst to dancing in cafés and nightclubs. In the 1950s the cafés didn't have a dance floor, so the hand jive, a choreographed form of hand movements, was invented so that people could "dance" along to the music emanating from the Rock-Ola machines. But as a total concept, the discotheque was a relatively new idea — in fact, only about ten years old — by the time I started to become a regular at the Bird's Nest.

"Discotheque" is a French word meaning "record library," and Paris is cited as the first city to have one. In 1953, torch singer turned nightclub owner Régine replaced the jukebox at her Whisky à Gogo club with two turntables, and with that the template for the modern discotheque was born.

There were two different strands of discotheque culture on either side of the Atlantic Ocean. In New York in the early 1960s, there were celebrity hangouts such as the Manhattan Club, the Peppermint Lounge (where the twist dance craze took off), and, later, Arthur, owned by Richard Burton's ex-wife Sybil Christopher. But it would be the American underground gay, black, and Latino nightclubs, and their pioneering DJs, in the early 1970s that would lay the foundation of what came to be known as disco music.

In the United Kingdom it was London's Soho district, already established as the centre of live music in the capital, where DJ culture was established in the 1960s. Afternoon dance parties were staged, and in the evenings DJs played records in between the sets of the live bands. Clubs such as Annabel's, The Scene (where the producers of *Ready Steady Go!* would recruit the coolest looking mods to appear on the TV show), Tiles, and particularly La Discotheque became gathering spots for the fashionable set, artists, and especially young mods. This was, after all, the beginning of the Swinging London era. La Discotheque became familiar to the British public when the club's name appeared in many scandalous news items between 1963 and 1965. The *Times* even referred to it as the centre of the "purple hearts" drug scene. The bouncers at the club were ex-boxers and ex-wrestlers, and one incident made headlines when one of the doormen was shot in the knee. A young Marc Bolan (of T. Rex) worked in the cloakroom.

One of the most famous clubs outside the capital was the Twisted Wheel in Manchester, which ran from 1963 through to 1971. It held all-night dance parties. Live acts would take the stage at 2:00 a.m., and the doors would close at 7 a.m. It gained a reputation, as did other clubs in the north, for playing "rare soul" — records imported from the United States — that clubs in the south of England were not playing. In 1970 music journalist Dave Godin dubbed it "Northern Soul." This laid the foundation for a whole "soul boy" culture that, beginning in 1973, centred on the all-night disco at Wigan Casino, fifty miles from Manchester.

Fashion was an incredibly important part of the culture, particularly if you were a regular club-goer. People could instantly tell what your interests, attitude, and social standing were by the clothes you wore.

The skinheads morphed into suedeheads — they grew their hair slightly longer, hence the name, but they still wore dark blue Crombie overcoats or sporty Harrington jackets, two-tone tonic suits, tongued and tasselled loafer shoes, Levi's Sta-Prest pants, and Ben Sherman shirts. If the DJ played a song that was popular on the football terraces, such as the ska tune "Liquidator" by Harry J. All Stars, sections of the clientele would break out into the chant of their favourite football team and you would know whose patch you were on. But just at this time, in the early seventies, glam rock was starting to emerge, with such artists as T. Rex ("Bang a Gong"), the Sweet ("Wig-Wam Bam"), Alice Cooper ("School's Out"), and Slade ("Cum On Feel the Noize"), who had started life as a skinhead band and had evolved into one of the United Kingdom's most successful groups. And as the music changed, so did the fashion. Guys wore Oxford bag pants, brightly coloured shirts, sleeveless sweaters, suit jackets, and platform shoes. Hairstyles for men were crucial — modelled on the Bay City Rollers, Bowie, or Rod Stewart. The girls were just as colourful — smock dresses, tank tops, very tall platform shoes, Chelsea girl hairstyles, and glitter under the eyes.

Disco, as a musical style, had not yet been born. The variety of music in U.K. nightclubs reflected the mixed crowd. DJs programmed the hits of the day, along with a soul repertoire, and Tamla Motown was usually the backbone of that soul playlist — there were the classic mid-sixties hits by the Four Tops, the Supremes, Jimmy Ruffin, and numerous other artists who defined one of the most successful labels in music history. In the early seventies there was the Jackson Five and Stevie Wonder's *Talking Book* album, with the incredible track "Superstition," and if you flicked through a friend's bedroom LP collection you invariably saw one of the many *Motown Chartbusters* compilations. (By 1972, seven different *Chartbusters* volumes had been released in the U.K.) Then a new soul arrangement, lush and more orchestrated, began to emerge to rival Motown and the musical city of Detroit. It was the Philadelphia sound.

Early in the 1970s the Philadelphia group the Stylistics had a string of hits with dreamy romantic ballads, including "You Are Everything," "Betcha by Golly, Wow," and "Break Up to Make Up." Those songs were all written by Thom Bell and Linda Creed, who were also from the City of Brotherly Love. But that was just a hint of what was going on. The musical spotlight fell on the city when writer-producers Kenny Gamble and Leon Huff established Philadelphia International Records (mirroring exactly what Berry Gordy had done with Motown Records). The label's, and Gamble and Huff's, success is one of the great musical stories of the era. They defined a sound and pointed the way to what would eventually be defined as disco music. Their hits in the first three years of operation include "Back Stabbers" and "Love Train" by the O'Jays, "If You Don't Know Me By Now" by Harold Melvin and the Bluenotes, "Me and Mrs. Jones" by Billy Paul, and "TSOP (The Sound of Philadelphia)" by MFSB, which became the theme song for the city and the TV show *Soul Train*. One song by Gamble and Huff in particular resonated with me: "Year of Decision" by the Three Degrees. The title summed up my life at that moment.

# CHAPTER 4

# Trouble

Even though I was in my last year of school, I thought little of my future. I was having too much fun totally immersed in music and club life, and on Saturday afternoons cheering on Fulham Football Club from the Hammersmith End of the Craven Cottage ground. What little money I had would finance this lifestyle, and with whatever was left over I would buy records — seven-inch singles in particular. I began to catalogue them, not in alphabetical order of the artist's name but of the label, starting with the letter *A* for Apple all the way to *W* for Warner Brothers. Even now, that seems such a strange thing to do, but I was beguiled by pop music and fascinated by its industry. Before I went to bed at night I would stack four or five of my favourite singles on the automatic spindle of the turntable. The record player was on the shelf at the head of my bed, and in the morning, with sleep still in my eyes, I would reach up and press "play" and the songs would keep me company as I washed and dressed for school. (We had no shower in those days. It was a bath once a week.) By the time I made it downstairs and took my place at the regular spot at the breakfast table, I would have a smile on my face, ready to start the day. But my happy-go-lucky attitude and my constant clubbing annoyed my serious and disciplined father. He wanted to know what I was going to do with my life. I had no idea.

This was still an England governed by a class system and tradition. Even though things had started to change by the early seventies, at its foundation there was still the belief that one should know one's place and stick to it. Life was routine, and still fairly austere. Punctually at 7:45 a.m. my father left for work. If I was ready in time I would join him, and we would take our place in the traffic jam of cars crawling their way into the heart of the city, listening to Tony Blackburn's *Breakfast Show* on Radio 1. This was not a world I wanted to be part of. I also did not expect to go to university or college, which a large proportion of the students at Latymer were destined to do. For those of us caught between a world of academia and factory work, the opportunities were slim. And so the school organized a careers day (which parents had to pay for), and advisers were appointed to have one-on-one interviews with the students. It was very depressing. My form master wrote a letter to my father explaining that I apparently "exhibited little interest in trying to find suitable employment." He went on to say that this was "not a condemnation of the boy" but that my father should be aware of the situation, as he had paid for the services. My dad never got to read that letter, as I managed to get to it first when it was delivered by the postman.

It did not help matters that on one particular occasion all the sixth form boys were assembled in the Great Hall to listen to a guest speaker. I can't remember who the speaker was, or what the presentation was about. I fell asleep. The headmaster happened to be sitting a couple of rows back and saw me snoozing. Of course, my schoolmates thought this was hilarious. The headmaster did not share their view. The following day I was called into his study (an ominous sign at the best of times). Caning — "six of the best" — was not usually used as punishment at Latymer, but it always crossed your mind. (Corporal punishment was not outlawed in British schools until 1986.) The headmaster wanted to know why I had fallen asleep, what my lifestyle was like, and was I always "determined to be bored." I had no clever answers.

Mick had left school at fifteen, lived with his sister and her husband, and had a job in a men's boutique in Richmond. Not just any boutique, but the famous Ivy Shop, which, in the mid-sixties, was the place to buy mod gear. It became top spot for the skinheads to buy their clobber, particularly the Harrington jacket (which the Ivy Shop named and popularized), button-down collared shirts, and Sta-Prest pants; in short, the skinhead uniform. By 1973 the shop's fashion catered to the suave male frequenting the football ground in the afternoon and the disco at night. Mick's weekly brown envelope of cash wasn't substantial, but the regular pay gave him the opportunity to buy stylish, expensive clothes with an employee discount. He had his mind set on eventually becoming a brickie — a bricklayer. The money was better, and, as he said, being outside gave him the chance to get a tan. But right now he was just happy to have a job during tough times. As the only one of us working, he was able to spring for a few more beers than me. But I didn't mind as I was the designated driver. And of course the stylish car, even though it was my dad's, impressed the girls.

As 1973 began, my future was as unclear as a foggy January day. My final exams would take place in June, and I still had no clue what I wanted to do with my life. Becoming a radio DJ would have been my dream, but back then that was an impossibility. Remarkable as it seems now, the U.K. still had only one radio network, the BBC, and their DJs were all mostly graduates of pirate radio: Ed Stewart, Johnnie Walker, and Kenny Everett. There was no way that I was going to get a look in. (The United Kingdom's first independent commercial pop station, Capital Radio, did not go on the air till October 1973.) University was not an option, even if I did manage to pass my three A-level exams. I had had enough of learning. The only thing I did know was that I wanted adventure, and I wanted to find that adventure in Canada.

I had no idea why Canada. Maybe it was in my DNA. There was a connection to the country. My father, a Royal Air Force pilot who had completed his training in Ontario and become part of Ferry Command during the war years, had met my mother, an American journalist, in Montreal and was married in the city just before the war ended. They settled back in England in the suburbs of my dad's hometown of London in 1946. But their romantic history was not the reason I had Canada in mind. Nor was it the fact that my eldest brother, Waynne, and his new wife had moved to Nova Scotia in 1969, after being hired by the provincial government. I had wanderlust and wanted out of England, which, as my father said, "seemed to be going down the plughole" with its economic problems, labour strikes, and hooliganism, as well as the Troubles in Northern Ireland. The previous year was a particularly bad one. On January 30, 1972, British troops killed fourteen people when they fired on demonstrators in Derry ("Sunday Bloody Sunday," as U2 would later sing), and a few days later the British Embassy in Dublin was burnt down. Back in England, an IRA bomb killed six people at Aldershot barracks, the first of a series of explosions that terrorized England for the next couple of years. In February of that year, a state of emergency was declared over the miner's strike, which lasted seven weeks. A couple of months later, British dockers went on strike. Another state of emergency was declared. The U.K. unemployment rate exceeded over a million people for the first time since the 1930s, and at the beginning of 1973, the U.K. lost its independence when it joined the Common Market (later the European Union). Now was a good time to leave.

I wasn't the only one in my family wishing to leave England. My brother Basil had applied for, and been granted, a U.S. Green Card that would allow him to live and work in the States. Late in February 1973, a small going-away party was organized for him. About a dozen friends and family started off the party at our local pub in the High Street, The Rising Sun, and then after a couple of pints of beer everyone made their way to our house — all except Mick, who was going to go to the Bird's Nest to meet a couple of girls and bring them back to the party. One of my other friends in attendance at the farewell was my schoolmate Barry. He had just bought a full-length black leather coat in Petticoat Lane, a London east-end market known for bargains. The coat was the height of fashion. It was something you would see one of the new glam rock musicians, such as the Sweet, wear on *Top of the Pops*. Mick wanted to borrow it for an hour or two, and he would return it once he got back to the party. However, he never made it back in time, or in one piece.

Back at the house the guests came and went, and still no Mick. At about two o'clock in the morning, with just my brother, my friend Barry (waiting for his coat), and I still awake, cleaning up after the party, the doorbell rang. "That'll be Mick," I said, "late as usual." I opened the door to a horrific sight. There standing in front of me under the porch light was my best friend, badly beaten up — bloodied, bandaged, and in a terrible state. The full-length black leather coat that he had borrowed was covered in dried blood on one side, from the collar all the way to the ankle. Tearfully, he recounted what had happened. While at the Bird's Nest, some local lads had convinced him to meet them outside to discuss "things." The coat had given Mick a swagger that obviously these blokes didn't appreciate. In the darkness of the club parking lot, six of them jumped him and kicked his face in so badly the bone in his nose was almost touching his brain. He had barely escaped with his life. Running down the street, he had spotted a police car with two coppers inside. (They regularly parked outside the Bird's Nest in anticipation of Saturday night trouble. There was another bar opposite, Henekey's, and sometimes there would be pitched battles in the middle of Twickenham Junction as the two sets of drunken patrons clashed at closing time.) Mick jumped into the back seat, pleading for help. The gang ran away, and the cops took Mick to the hospital, where he was patched up. An ambulance drove him to our house. Trouble had eventually found Mick. It was a sad end to the night and Basil's last days in England.

Mick later told me that the individual who had initiated the fight and led the pack of bovver boys who beat him up was Freddie, the skinhead who had joined me and Barry on that walk home from Richmond for his added protection just a couple of months previously.

# CHAPTER 5

# The Interview

It was my father, in one of those rare moments when we were actually talking to each other, who suggested I apply to the Hudson's Bay Company. His mention of the name conjured up images of Canada in the nineteenth century: fur traders, canoes, and aboriginal people in traditional garb — was he joking? Surely it was as dead as that old dodo bird. As it turns out, "The Bay," as it was known at that time, was a dominant force in Canadian retail and still had trading posts in the Canadian North. Dad gave me their address — 77 Main Street, Winnipeg, Manitoba — and I wrote them a letter in my best handwriting. I hoped I might impress them with my ambition for adventure, as I had no resumé of any significance. Within a couple of weeks I received an answer. By coincidence, the Company was in the middle of an annual hiring campaign in "the old country" — selecting about ten young adventurers to work in the Northern Stores department. Could I attend an interview at Beaver House, their London office? Full of enthusiasm, I phoned the number embossed on the stylish letterhead and confirmed my appointment.

The day of the interview I cut classes at Latymer, telling my schoolmates what I was up to, and caught the tube from Ravenscourt Park into the city. I arrived an hour early just to make sure I could locate Beaver House in Great Trinity Lane. Once I knew where the building was, I retreated to a nearby Lyons tea room (there was no Starbucks in those days) to kill time and think about what I was going to say to the person who might hire me. Five minutes before the appointed hour, I made my way to the historic building. The Company's coat of arms, flanked on either side by images of two huge stags, was mounted over the doorway. A serious-looking doorman in an official-looking uniform approached me and asked me my business. I explained I was there for an interview. He checked my name on a list pinned to his brown clipboard. Yes, I was expected. A receptionist led me down a wide corridor. On either side were impressive large oil portraits — images of some of the Company's famous men, dating back to the seventeenth century. I was walking through history.

Even all these years later, there are a number of things I clearly remember about the interview. First, the chap who interviewed me was Ed Spracklin — a veteran of the Northern Stores department. His face had the grizzled look of a man who had endured a hard environment. He looked as if he would have been more at home hunting timber wolves than future employees. Second, he asked me if I wanted a cup of tea. I said yes, a woman rolled in a tea trolley, and I was served tea in a delicate pink china cup and saucer and offered a biscuit. (It occurred to me that this charming gesture was the epitome of the highbrow British society that I was doing my best to escape.) He then told me about the Company, its rich past, and its glamorous present with huge department stores that anchored the downtown core of every Canadian city. His career had started off as a clerk, and later a manager, for the company in such places as Repulse Bay and Baker Lake. He explained that the Northern Stores department was a separate division that grew out of the trading posts of yesteryear. They were small general stores that sold almost everything that you would expect to find in any retail outlet down south, but they catered to an indigenous population. In many of the outposts, fur trading was still an important source of revenue: seal, fox, wolf, and beaver pelts.

Mr. Spracklin then asked me a series of questions: What were my favourite subjects at school? History and sports, I replied. What was my least favourite? French, I said without hesitation. I was a terrible French student. In fact, I was so disruptive that the teacher told me to sit at the back of the room and read *Melody Maker* rather than participate in the class. And then he asked me, "Do you lead, or do you like to follow?" "I don't follow anybody, and I don't expect anybody to follow me. I go my own way," I replied. I have no idea where that lucid thought came from, but the answer seemed to satisfy him. He then spread out a large map of Canada on top of his desk. It was the first time I had ever had a close look at the country. There were a series of red dots marked across the top of the map. Each of these dots represented a Company outpost. If I was hired, where would I like to be posted? There were such names as Red Sucker Lake, Norway House, and Rankin Inlet. *Well*, I thought, *if I'm going to go, let's go all the way.* So I pointed to the single red dot that was furthest north on the map — Igloolik, a place deep in the Canadian Arctic. This action would later play a significant role in my future.

After about an hour the interview was concluded, and I left Beaver House with the belief that I would not be hired, particularly after my comment about not liking French, Canada's other official language. Back at school, the rumour had gone around that I had applied for a job with this historic company and the old joke "I was going to sell fridges to the Eskimos" was resurrected at my expense. How true that turned out to be.

With my days as a schoolboy winding down, I gave one last concerted effort to at least attempt to pass my final exams. It was a tough go. I would sit at my bedroom desk trying to catch up on all the studying I had not done and wonder how mathematical statistics and the gradient of a curve were going to help me with my adult life. I was more interested in Marvin Gaye's soulful album *What's Goin' On* than I was in my soulless New Math textbook. But I stuck with it, and that June I sat my three A-level exams (geography, history, and mathematics). I thought I might have at least scraped through two of them. Math was a writeoff; the only gradient on that curve was straight down. After the final exam I walked through the school gates for the last time with a sense of freedom. Latymer had been a constant in my life for almost ten years, ever since I was a nine-year-old in the prep department. But there was no graduation dance or final farewell, and everyone drifted off in different directions — in the words of the poet T.S. Eliot, it ended "not with a bang but a whimper."

Regardless of my exam results, my dad was thrilled that I had at least completed school. As a reward, he booked a two-week holiday for Mick and me in Benidorm, Spain, which at that time was fast becoming the party destination for young Europeans with the so-called "package holidays." Modern discotheques were one of the new attractions, as

Me, Saturday night before the disco.

well as the warm weather and beaches. Mick didn't have any money (or parents to help him out), so it was a gift for him as well.

We arrived at the Costa Blanca resort full of excitement in late June. It was warm and sunny, and the hotel was by the beach. There were lots of girls. And the place was alive with youthful energy. In the bright, modern hotel we met up with eight guys from Glasgow, slightly older than us, who had all booked off vacation time from their factory jobs so that they could party together. We met two beautiful girls who had the room next to ours. They were our age — eighteen — but, of course, looking for older guys with money, so Mick and I knew we had no chance with them.

The days were spent at the beach, the nights at the clubs. Sightseeing was not on the hit list, and certainly no bullfights. About a week into the holiday Mick and I were at a nearby disco. The two girls from our hotel were there as well. We exchanged hellos but did not stop to chat. Later on that evening the girls were being bothered by a group of skinheads. In order to get away from the six or so bovver boys, they came and sat on the couches next to us in the corner. We made small talk and, needless to say, were happy for the attention. Within a couple of minutes the skinheads came to where we were sitting. Holding their pint mugs and standing in front of us in an intimidating way, they started mouthing off. They were Geordies, from Newcastle in the north of England, and we were the hated Londoners.

Suddenly, one of them accidentally-on-purpose tipped his beer on me. "Hey, you spilt my beer. You cunt — you owe me," he snarled in his thick accent.

One of the girls stood up from the couch, grabbed my hand, and said, "Come on, we're leaving."

I went to stand up. The next thing I remember was a fist landing straight in my face. My nose shattered, blood all over the place. Mick started throwing punches. The remaining Geordies jumped on top of us. The girls started screaming. Just at that moment our new

Scottish friends were at the top of the stairs in the disco. Six of them came charging down and joined the fight. There was a cluster of bodies punching and kicking in the middle of the dance floor. The whole place had stopped to watch this mess unfold. Blood was pouring down my face. Like a scene out of a Charlie Chaplin movie, I somehow managed to crawl out of the knot of bodies on my hands and knees. A big, burly bouncer grabbed me by the scruff of the neck and threw me out the back door, as if I had been the instigator. Mick followed soon after. Later, back in the hotel, after I had cleaned up, we met the girls, who apologized for the trouble, and the Scots guys. We thanked them for their help, and for the remainder of the holiday partied together every night, drinking Pernod and dancing in the open-air discotheques to classic Tamla Motown records.

The letter was waiting for me on the hall table when I returned home. I had been offered a job of "clerk in training" in the Northern Stores department. There was also another letter — my exam results. I had passed geography and history with the lowest passing grade possible. But at least I had passed, and besides, the exams were now irrelevant. I was off to Canada! I wrote back to the Company accepting the position. They responded with a contract that started off with the words "The Governor and Company of Adventurers of England, trading into Hudson's Bay ..." It was all very official and something out of the British Museum. I signed the paperwork, and my future was set.

The remaining days were spent in preparation for my departure. My dad bought me a new, large, sturdy suitcase and a second-hand Yashica camera, and presented me with one hundred pounds in cash. My mom organized new socks and underwear, knitted me a new black-and-white Fulham football scarf, and dug out from the closet an old brown schoolboy duffel coat. Normally, I would not have been seen dead in such an unfashionable item, but it was the only thing in the house that might possibly keep me warm on cold Arctic nights. (How wrong we

Form N.S.1A-U.K.

**This Agreement** made in triplicate this ____13____ day of ___September___ 19__7_

BETWEEN

**The Governor and Company of Adventurers of England
Trading into Hudson's Bay**

herein called "The Company"

OF THE FIRST PART

AND

KIM CHAMPNISS

herein called "The Employee,"

OF THE SECOND PART

WITNESSETH that in consideration of the mutual agreements herein the parties agree as follows:

1. The Employee will serve the Company in its Northern Stores Department at such place as the

Company or its officers shall direct from the ___THIRTIETH___ day of ___SEPTEMBER___ 19_73_

until this agreement is terminated, in the capacity of ___Clerk in Training___
and in such other capacity as the Company or its Officers shall from time to time direct, and will diligently, honestly and faithfully perform all such work and services as he shall be required or directed to perform by its Officers, and will obey all rules and regulations now or hereafter made by the Company applicable to his employment, and will not during his period of employment engage or be concerned directly or indirectly in any trade or employment whatsoever except for the benefit of the Company and according to its orders.

2. The Employee's remuneration shall be $4,800 (Four thousand eight hundred dollars)

Dollars per annum to be computed from the ___30th___ day of ___September___ 19__7_
(or date of embarkation)

3. The present policies, rules and regulations of the Northern Stores Department are in the Handbook for Employees issued in 1969, and the Employee is entitled to the rights and privileges therein set forth not inconsistent herewith, and subject to repeal, cancellation, amendment or change as the said Northern Stores Department may from time to time in its discretion make.

4. This agreement may be terminated at any time by either party giving to the other ___one___
___month's___ notice in writing to that effect, or by the Company at its option paying to the Employee his salary for a like period in lieu of such notice. Such notice shall be given by the Employee to the officer in charge of his Store, District or Department.

5. If this agreement should be terminated by the Employee under the above provision before

he has completed ___two___ years of service, the Company will not pay any return transportation expenses, but the same shall be borne by the Employee.

6. On completion of two years of service, the Company will refund to the employee the cost of his transportation from the United Kingdom to Canada.

7. This contract cancels all existing contracts between the parties and contains the entire agreement between them, and the Employee does not rely on any representations, verbal or written, made to him before entering into this contract.

For the HUDSON'S BAY COMPANY

Witness ___M. Paul___

Hudson's Bay Company employment contract.

were.) As for me, I retrieved my prized sheepskin-lined leather motor-cycle boots purchased the year I rode my BSA C15. I thought they, too, would keep me warm. (Once again, how wrong I was.)

With my parents' permission I organized a going-away party. I wanted it to be memorable. And it was. I typed up a simple invitation with BBB (blokes bring a bottle) at the bottom, photocopied a stack of them, and handed them out at the Bird's Nest and at my brother's work, where I had a temporary job for the summer. I sent them to school friends, biker pals, ex-girlfriends, and neighbours who had known me almost all my life. I even sent them to the Scottish guys who had come to my rescue in Spain. I booked a mobile DJ. (We had to have a DJ.) The day of the party, Mick, some friends, and I helped clear out the living room to make way for the DJ and the guests. The furniture was assigned to the garage. My mother was excited about the whole event. The house had not seen a big party for some years. But my father was having a moment of parental crisis. His hot blood was rising rapidly like thermometer mercury. I thought he was going to blow his top. He strategically said he was going to the office and wouldn't be back till late. It was a Saturday. He hadn't been to the office on the weekend in years. It was, however, a tactful and appreciated move.

After all the organization and the arrival of the mobile DJ, the scene was set. I had arranged to meet the Scottish guys, who were coming down from Glasgow, at Piccadilly Circus tube station in the late afternoon. Six of them arrived on time, but already they were three sheets to the wind. We made our way back to the house somehow. By then, the first guests were beginning to arrive. Soon, the whole house was packed — bikers, dancers, old girlfriends, school chums. There must have been over a hundred people in the house, and the guests spilled out into the front and back gardens. Cars and bikes filled the road; laughter and music filled the air. The breakfast room became the bar, and the multitude of bottles that the guests had bought were stacked up along the wall. We were not going to run out of booze, that was for sure. The DJ was great. The party was a spectacular success. My father returned just in time to see one of my biker friends puking over his prize roses. What timing! Luckily, there was no damage to the house, and thank goodness it was an age before cellphones and social media. I can only imagine what would have happened if I had planned the party in this modern age. The only potential negative incident was a gang of troublemakers who arrived looking for Mick but were unable to find him and left without incident. I'm not sure where he went, but he may have got word they were looking for him.

Days before my departure, Mick and I borrowed my Dad's car for the final time to travel down to Eastbourne on the south coast to say goodbye to my grandmother. It was a two-hour drive and I remember the song "Year of Decision" by the Three Degrees being played on the radio constantly. We spent the afternoon with my grandmother and took her out for a drive, visiting Beachy Head and enjoying the brisk wind and the spectacular view of the English Channel. That evening we planned to visit Brighton, the party capital just up the coast. We ended up at an extremely large club called Sherry's that had a huge dance floor and a long bar (I think one of the longest in England). A balcony encircled the venue, allowing great sightlines of the club and its patrons. We were enjoying ourselves immensely, and then the DJ announced that there would be a dance contest. It turns out that was one of the regular features of the club. With encouragement from Mick, I entered the event, and of all things, I won! The prize — free beers and a red plastic suitcase! The universe seemed to know my future.

On September 30, 1973, I, along with nine other young adventurers, arrived at the British Airways terminal in the heart of the city and were greeted by a Company employee who checked us in. I said my goodbyes to my family and to Mick. I was excited. They were sad. A bus took the ten of us to Heathrow, and we boarded a 747 jumbo jet for Canada and the start of a new life working for "The Governor and Company of Adventurers of England, trading into Hudson's Bay ..."

# CHAPTER 6

# Canada

After a long journey, the ten of us found ourselves in the Fort Garry Hotel near the Company's Canadian head office in Winnipeg. After the nightlife of London, Winnipeg was a shock. It was as exciting as a 1950s doctor's waiting room. It harkened back to a forgotten era, a time when Winnipeg was "the gateway to the North." Even some of its laws were from another time. In the bars, we discovered that you could not stand up with your beer; if you wanted to change tables, a waitress had to carry your drink to your new seat.

On our second day there, the ten of us made our way to the Company head office. I was wearing my fashionable London clothes: platform shoes, Oxford bag trousers, and a thin thread of colourful love beads around my neck. As we passed some local young people, they stared at me — not in a bad way, but a "look at that silly fellow" kind of way. I remember shouting out, "I'm only bloody English!" It would not take too many weeks in Canada to knock the fashion victim out of me. Over the next couple of days we were given a crash course in fur buying (did you know that one of the unique ingredients for perfume comes from the scrotum of the beaver?) and basic bookkeeping, and a dental checkup, because if you get a toothache in the Canadian wilderness you have to endure the pain until you can be shipped out. I remember the Company dentist being extremely elderly. He asked me where I was from, and I told him London. He said he loved the city and had happy memories of being there after the war. "What did you do during the Second World War?" I asked. "Oh no, the First World War," he said.

One by one each of us then met up with Ed Spracklin again. We were assigned our posts. All but me were going to the Canadian bush to work in the stores on the First Nations reserves. I was posted to the Far North in a place called Eskimo Point in the Keewatin district of the Northwest Territories. Mr. Spracklin apologized that he couldn't find me an opening in Igloolik (the red dot I had originally pointed to during the initial interview), but he thought I might like this settlement on the west coast of Hudson Bay.

Eskimo Point, now known as Arviat.
© 2006. Her Majesty the Queen in Right of Canada, Natural Resources Canada.

The following day I boarded a small jet bound for Churchill, Manitoba, a town in the north of the province. From there I was to board another plane for Eskimo Point. It occurred to me that the planes were getting smaller and smaller the farther I travelled into the heart of the country. And the farther north I went, the more I seemed to be going back in time. In anticipation of my first blast of extreme weather, I wore that much-despised brown duffle coat, my Fulham football scarf, and the sheepskin-lined leather motorcycle boots. At least my legs and feet would be warm, I rationalized. Silly me.

Waiting in the lounge at the Churchill Airport, things started to turn, shall we say, unusual. It was my first glimpse of an "Eskimo" woman, as we said then. She was crouched on her haunches in the corner and was rocking back and forth. She wore a traditional white smock dress that had an oversized hood. In that hood was a baby. It was a wonderful sight to see, but what made it bizarre was that the old woman was blowing huge pink bubbles with the gum she chewed. Every now and then the bubble burst, and the baby would laugh at the silliness. I would learn later that "Eskimo" was a term these people did not like, as it was said to mean "eater of raw meat." They preferred to be called "Inuit," which means "the people." It was indicative of a change in attitude and in the political awareness of indigenous people. But that word had not yet become commonly accepted, and it was rarely used at the time, other than by the Inuit themselves and those concerned with aboriginal rights and culture.

Occasionally, the lounge door would slam open, pushed by the strong wind, and someone would enter, looking radically different from anyone I would have seen back home: hunters in fringe jackets and mukluks, heavily padded construction workers with oversized gloves and boots, and Inuit families. I then realized that, once again, everyone was looking at me. It was I who was different — not them.

"You a new Bay boy?" the airline rep asked. Bay boy — it was the first time I had heard the term, but it wouldn't be the last.

"Yes," I replied, "I'm on my way to Eskimo Point," I said proudly. He smiled knowingly and told me my plane was ready to board.

I walked out to the Transair DC3, which was parked on the cold, windy runway like a fat duck ready to take flight. Its front end was much higher than its back end, and it looked like it would leap into the grey sky at any moment. I climbed the metal stairs into the body of the aircraft. This was no sleek machine. It looked like it was left over from the Second World War. There appeared to be gaffer tape covering holes in the side. It was cold. There was no carpet on the floor, just naked, bare steel. At the back of the plane I could see all the freight kept in place by a rope net: Coleman stoves, cabbages, potatoes, my dark blue suitcase, and all kinds of assorted items headed north into the Arctic.

A flight attendant wearing a parka told me to move up the aisle and find a seat. It was a fairly steep incline up to the top of the plane, and the steel trimming on the soles and heels of my motorcycle boots, which had made sense on the streets of London, allowed me no grip on the steel floor of the plane. They slipped like ice on ice. I had to "paddle" my way up the aisle using the armrests. I settled into my seat and watched the noisy propeller engines spin to life. The plane inched ahead, and then hurtled down the runway. With a lurch the clumsy metal bird took to the sky. Just at that moment a part of the rope cage at the back of the plane broke free, and cabbages and parcels came rolling down the gangway. Quickly, the flight attendant gathered them up and re-secured the netting as best as she could. As the plane headed north, I looked down and could see nothing but flat tundra as we flew past the tree line. Eighty miles north of this line was Eskimo Point. It was close to the geographical centre of Canada. Not only was I taking the classic path to the New World, but I also was moving to almost the exact middle of the country.

Universal circumstance was playing a cosmic joke upon me.

# CHAPTER 7

# Eskimo Point

The Transair DC3 landed on a gravel runway in the middle of nowhere. Rusty forty-five-gallon drums were the only welcoming committee. The cabbages, Coleman stoves, and numerous parcels, including royal blue sacks of mail, were off-loaded. So was I. The plane's cargo door slammed shut and its propellers spun to life, and with an about-turn the DC3 roared down the runway and left me to silence and an endless flat horizon. I looked around and could see small buildings about a mile away. I sat on my suitcase and waited. After a short while, a dusty blue pickup truck grated down the gravel runway and stopped close by. Two Inuit men stepped out, looked at me, said nothing, and began to load the freight. They then, again without saying anything, directed me to sit in back amongst the cardboard boxes, the majority of which were all plainly labelled with the yellow Company logo. I, too, had become freight for the Company. After a bumpy ride the truck pulled up at the store, located at the heart of the settlement. I had arrived.

The building was busier than Oxford Street at Christmastime. Inuit men and women in traditional costumes were buying enormous quantities of everything available. Children with runny noses and loud voices were screaming and running around. Hunters were carrying fur

The Eskimo Point Hudson's Bay store.

Ralph King, Hudson's Bay manager, in the office at the store.

pelts, and some were examining rifles. I made my way to the back of the store, where I spotted someone who appeared to be in charge. His black hair was slicked back like Elvis's, he had a huge pot belly, and he had a pipe in his mouth, which wasn't lit but it was upside down. He also had a friendly face.

"Ralph King? Hi, I'm your new clerk."

Ralph looked at me with amazement. I must have looked ridiculous in my duffle coat, Fulham football scarf, and motorcycle boots. My hair was styled like that of Aladdin Sane, the character image of David Bowie's latest album, my favourite record at the time.

"Did you just step off the boat?"

"No, I came by plane," I responded, not understanding the joke.

Silence.

"I've no time for you now. The welfare cheques have arrived. Take your stuff to the staff house and get settled." The manager turned away and shouted in the direction of a backroom: "Doug!"

In walked a tall, stocky youth.

"Doug, you've got a new roommate. Show him where to go."

Doug looked at me disapprovingly. I knew he wanted to tell me where to go. "Okay. Follow me," and the two of us set off through the crowd of shoppers and out to the staff house, which was about fifty yards away. Like all the other buildings owned by the Company, it was painted red and white. This was to be my home for the next year.

Just one week earlier, I had been in a Brighton discotheque that had more people in it than the whole of this community. Instead of dodging groups of violent youths, I was now dodging mud puddles in Eskimo Point. Looking back, the only way I can describe it is like that scene in the movie *The Deer Hunter* where Robert De Niro's character goes from the rambunctious wedding reception party in his Midwestern hometown to the jungles of Vietnam in a split second. It was that radical. Luckily, I didn't have to run from bullets.

The red-and-white staff house was situated just forty feet from the open water of Hudson Bay. It was modern and only a couple of years old, and we each had our own room. I was apparently lucky because the previous staff house, which was still standing next door and now being used to store gasoline, was a large, open one-room affair with a stove in the centre and the beds in the corners. It would have been like living on a submarine. For the new staff house, water, which was drawn from the surrounding lakes, was delivered once a week and pumped into a big tank by the front door. When the lakes were frozen, the truck delivered huge blocks of ice. The water had a brown stain to it, and we had to boil it before we used it. You could smell the kettle steaming. The stove was run on propane, and two large cylinders were housed in a little shed situated outside beside the kitchen window. There were two light bulbs, constantly switched on to emit heat, mounted beside the propane tanks to stop the gas from freezing. But sometimes they still froze, and Doug would be out there with wrench in hand, hammering away out of frustration. I remember once he became so angry with his inability to get the gas fitting secure that he turned around and hurled the wrench as far as he could, like a boomerang. But it didn't come back. We had to search for the tool in the snow to get the propane stove working, or there would be no supper that night.

There wasn't any underground plumbing, as the permafrost would freeze pipes. The toilet was a honey bucket lined with an extra-strong plastic bag. The first time that it was my turn to empty the bucket, I twist-tied the bag, trying my best not to breathe in the fumes, pulled it out, and carried it at arm's length through the staff house on my way to dump it in the forty-five-gallon drum outside, which acted as a garbage can. Doug started yelling at me: "Stupid! Watch out!" I should not have carried the bag by itself, but should have left it in the inner bucket, which had a handle I couldn't see. Luckily, the bag was as good as its name — extra-strong Glad.

I remember the first time I volunteered to make coffee for Doug and some visitors to the staff house. I was a tea drinker in England. My family drank coffee, and we always had a large jar of instant Maxwell House handy. Any time I made coffee for my parents or my brothers, I just took a teaspoonful of granules for each cup, poured in the hot water, and stirred the contents. In Eskimo Point, I entered the kitchen, searched for the coffee jar, saw a tin marked with "COFFEE," spooned in a teaspoonful of the stuff into each of the mugs, boiled the water, and served it up. "Yuck" was the response from Doug and our guests. Epic failure. I had spooned in ground beans used for a percolating coffee maker instead of instant granules. I had no idea there was a difference. I learned quickly after that. In fact, I started drinking coffee for the first time ever.

Doug was from Winnipeg. He was a born outdoorsman, and spent many nights cleaning his rifle and sharpening his hunting knife. He was also a keen hockey player, and had the short fuse to match. We

Doug Moore, who loved to hunt.

were dramatically different, but we got along. You had to, as there was nowhere else to go. No trees to hide behind. No pub in which to drown your sorrows — in fact, Eskimo Point was a "dry settlement," and booze was not permitted. Just one or two people you might be able to visit.

All of the Inuit young people spoke English, but not so for many of the elders. I had to learn to communicate in a hurry. The two basic words of "yes" and "no" were covered with facial expressions: if it was a positive response, the eyebrows would be raised; if negative, then they would screw up their faces as if there was a bad smell. An Inuktitut word I learned in a hurry was *kabloona* — which meant "white man." I was told that it literally meant "hairy eyebrows" or "hairy face." That made sense. I noticed that Inuit men had very little facial hair. The locals gave me a nickname, *Titaraktitna*, which meant "little clerk." Doug, who was over six feet tall, was "big clerk." But ultimately, we were the Bay boys to everyone in the settlement, white or aboriginal. I had entered a long tradition of indoctrinating young men into the ways of the North, and their roles in being the individuals who made the economic engine of the settlement work effectively, efficiently, and profitably — the Hudson's Bay Company Trading Post.

Only seven hundred and fifty people lived in Eskimo Point, and fifty of these were the transient workers from the south: teachers, nurses, RCMP officers, government contractors, and Company employees. There was also one mysterious chap called Don who was rumoured to be an American draft dodger. The effects of the Vietnam War had reached this far north. He kept himself to himself and mixed only with the aboriginal community. There were no roads, rail connections, or trees; no television, no phone connection beyond the settlement, and only partial radio reception. The settlement's rhythms revolved around the weather, hunting, and the twice-weekly arrival of the airplane, which, like an Arctic fantasy island connection, brought supplies, welfare cheques, letters, and care packages from home. Ralph ordered *Reader's Digest* and *Time* magazine. This was the only way we received news of such things as the Vietnam War, Watergate, and the oil embargo. It was our only contact with the outside world. There was also a Company magazine that was distributed to the northern stores: the *Moccasin Telegraph*. It took its name from the idea that news and gossip travelled across the wilderness in the old days by word of mouth from indigenous people. The magazine reported on news from the outposts and had various articles of interest, but nothing of substance. However, with little else to read, it was regularly scanned from cover to cover, and for people like Ralph, it gave him a chance to keep track of other Company people he knew.

The only immediate way to contact the outside world was through an old shortwave radio left over from the 1950s upstairs at the store. If there was an urgent message to either send or receive, this was the only available option. The radio was kept on the whole time so that you could hear any messages aimed at Eskimo Point, and there was always the constant noise of static emanating from upstairs as Doug and I worked in the backroom pricing area. You would also hear the various messages being transmitted across the North to various outposts, which sometimes were fascinating and entertaining in their own way. I had to use the radio a couple of times to broadcast some messages. My distinctive London accent caused a bit of a startled reaction in those who heard it coming across the network. Scots, Newfie, or Canadian accents were the norm, not the voice of some young bloke from southwest London. *Who the hell was that?* was the response from various disembodied voices sitting at their stations deep in the Canadian wilderness. The radio wasn't the only thing left over from the old days up there. All kinds of Company paraphernalia from past decades were tucked in drawers, hidden in corners, or forgotten in boxes. There were lots of posters and flags from three years previous, all marked with a clever marriage of the dates 1670 and 1970 as a logo celebrating the three hundredth anniversary of the Company.

Ralph was a fine fellow and a Company man for life. He was a Newfoundlander and had been up North ever since he was a Bay boy. He had married an Inuit woman, Jackie, and they had two children. As such, he was particularly sensitive to aboriginal issues and the problems for all residents of northern settlements. He had a wonderful sense of humour, particularly if he was drinking from his own private stock of rum. He worked hard, and had a fatherly streak in him. He made sure that some of the first things I bought were a warm parka and a pair of snowmobile boots, which, naturally, were purchased at the store on my account. He encouraged me to buy a gun, a pump action .22, as I would need it for hunting, recreation, and possibly protection from wild animals. Everything I bought for the next year went on that account, and I soon realized that purchases whittled away at my meager wage. Not that I received any money in my hands. Where could I spend it? My wages were accumulating at the head office in Winnipeg

Me, outfitted for life in the North.

(less the cost of my air flight over from the U.K., and less the cost of my food and housing allowance). Yes, I was working for the Company.

The store sold everything from bullets to bread, from Stompin' Tom Connors records to Ski-Doos. It was just like working in any other general store, except the work routine was interrupted by the steady flow of hunters shuffling into the store with Arctic white fox, harbour seal, or long-haired wolf pelts slung over their shoulders. I had to learn to stock the shelves, price the goods, mop the floors, order supplies, and distinguish between high-quality and low-grade furs. One of the first things I was asked to do was help Louie Angalik and Timothy Taleriktok, two successful local hunters who worked in the store, stock groceries. Tea, Carnation canned milk, Pilot biscuits (a hardtack cracker), and flour were always being replenished on the shelves. Although they spoke little to me, they were always helpful in showing how things worked and quick to assist when needed. Bay boys came and went, but Louie and Timothy stayed in two of the few jobs available in the settlement. (Louis would go on to work for the Department of Education as a cultural and heritage adviser. In 2013 he was awarded the Order of Nunavut for initiatives to provide on-the-land rehabilitative programming for youth and adult offenders.)

Flour, which made bannock, had the highest turnover. It was stocked in what was called the "old warehouse." This cold, wooden, large structure down by the water's edge was one of the first buildings at Eskimo Point, built in 1919. To get there you walked through a historical labyrinth of Company properties. You had to go through the backroom storm doors, down a corrugated tunnel that connected the new store from the old store (which was now a warehouse for dry goods), through another set of storm doors that led to the outside, and down the well-worn embankment path that led to the drafty warehouse.

The flour was packed floor to ceiling with 100-pound sacks. There appeared to be enough to last for years (in fact, some of it had been there that long). I had seen Louie and Tim hoist the sacks on their shoulders and then march off to the store to stock the shelves. I thought I would be able to duplicate the effort with ease.

Well, lifting the sack from its embedded home of many years was no problem, but moving the burden above my London schoolboy shoulders was harder than I had imagined. I couldn't do it. I grappled with the beast, covering myself in the white dust, and try as I might, I couldn't bring it above chest height. Not to be outdone, I bear-hugged the sack and waddled out of the old building toward the store.

I was going uphill toward not only the rear of the old store but also the Arctic wind, blowing in from the bay ferociously. My legs buckled under the weight, and I staggered like a drunken rock star. I made it to the door, somehow managed to open it, and with my stature diminishing with every step, waddled along the steel tunnel to the back of the pricing area. By the time I arrived at the storm door, I was on my knees. Not wanting to loosen my grip, I used my head to bang on the door for Doug to open it. He heard the rap, went to the small window to see who was there, peered over the top, could see nothing, presumed it was the wind, and returned to marking new goods. Out of frustration, I head-butted the entrance harder. Doug jumped up and opened the door, and in I toppled, sending clouds of flour into the dry air. Amid howls of laughter, I picked up my task and dragged it to the grocery shelves. Tim and Louie laughed with affection and knowledge at the silliness of the *Titaraktitna*.

Occasionally I had to work the cash register when the local girls were absent. The first thing I noticed was a lack of pennies. Ralph explained that, because Eskimo Point was a "closed settlement," there was no input from other sources. All the coinage was kept in the self-contained circle of the community. The Inuit were like every other consumer on the planet and kept pennies in a jar on their kitchen counters, so the store would run short. At the cash register, Bazooka Joe bubble gum was used as a penny. If the change on a purchase was six cents, I was instructed to hand back a nickel and a bubble gum.

This resulted in a number of unique elements. People were always chewing gum and blowing bubbles, including elderly women. The sight of a senior in full traditional dress blowing a Bazooka Joe bubble and hearing the smack when it burst back upon her face was a sight to behold. Pink wads of used gum were everywhere — buried in the snow, stuck under counters, and most annoying of all, trodden into the linoleum floor of the store. Ralph told Doug and me that once a month we would have to mop the floors. The reason? Because when we became managers and delegated the task to our clerks, we would know what a horrible job it was. On those Friday evenings that found us with mop and pail, we cursed the practice of handing out so much gum as we attempted to scrape the stuff off. It occurred to me that the transaction of using bubble gum for money could also favour the buyer. I asked Ralph whether I should accept bubble gum as currency if someone came in to buy something and tried to pay with it. "Don't even give them the idea," was his response.

Hunting and trapping were the main financial resources of the settlement, with Arctic white fox being the primary fur in winter. We bought the pelts for about thirty dollars apiece. Ralph showed me some of the tricks the hunters would use to "dress up" the pelt. One of them was to rub flour over the fur to make it appear whiter than normal. So one of the first things you had to do when examining the fur was hold it up and give it a good shake. Usually, flour dust filled the office. Wolf pelts were worth about fifty dollars plus a bounty from the wildlife officer. Sometimes dog skins were brought into the store in the hope that we would mistake them for wolf. Ralph showed me how to spot the difference, but you could never be too sure. Many of the hunters had an ongoing debt with the Company, so before the cash for the fur was handed over I had to check the hunter's account. If he was in arrears, part of the money was used to pay off the debt. Every hunter had an account; his name was on a card where all the receipts were catalogued, as well as the financial history of his family, listed like a bank passbook. There was also a personality profile (a few succinct words of observation and assessment from previous Company managers, going back decades) listing whether he was a good financial risk, his qualities as a hunter, and any other pertinent information. When the hunting was bad, or sickness prevented the family from going out on the land, the Company could lend the family money to buy food or purchase traps or ammunition. Luckily, during my year in Eskimo Point, it was a bountiful harvest and there was an abundance of game, and a steady supply of rich furs made their way to the Hudson's Bay Post. With cash in hand, the hunter would then turn around and spend the money in the store, and the majority of the money would be back in the cash registers by the end of the day. In addition, a successful hunter could order big items from the Company catalogue (yes, even fridges!), and the Company would transport them in via the yearly ship.

There was one other source of income, and that was soapstone carving. One night, shortly after I arrived, there was a knock on the front door of the staff house. I answered the door, and there were two local teenagers. Did I want to buy these carvings? They showed me two small statues: one of a hunter, the other of a seal. "How much?" I asked. Ten or fifteen dollars, they said. That seemed an unusual way to do business, and then Doug shouted out: "Give them the fifteen, or else they won't come back." So I did. Some weeks later an Inuit elder, John Pangnark, came to the house. He wanted to know if we wanted to buy his unusual carving. It was a hefty thing. Unlike the traditional carvings, this was a large, abstract piece of soapstone — strange lines, shapes, and faces. It wasn't very attractive. Doug and I declined, and the man never came back. "I already bought one of his pieces," Doug said. "I use it as a doorstop." Years later, I discovered that John Pangnark was one of the most respected modern Inuit artists and his works could sell for twenty thousand dollars.

Even though Eskimo Point was a dry settlement, there was, in fact, some beer. The homemade kind. And the brewer who perfected the stuff was Tim McQuade. He was a blue collar government worker who made sure we all had fuel oil and that the electricity for the settlement worked properly. He also made sure we had our own personal "fuel" — beer. Tim and his wife Doris had been up North most of their working lives. Their three children were born in the North. Ralph, along with his Inuit wife Jackie, would make this their favourite Friday night "visit." We would join them on many evenings. The living quarters were upstairs, and Tim and Ralph would be there stretched out on brown plastic leather La-Z-Boy chairs, drinking the home brew, while the ladies were in the kitchen preparing whatever food was available that week. We would pass many a night listening to records — the Carpenters and the Grass Roots were popular in the McQuade house — and argue the merits of that month's batch. Invariably, we would hear small bangs from downstairs. It was the occasional bottle of beer over-fermenting and exploding. One of the things I remember is Doris making mock apple pie out of Ritz crackers (there was, of course, no fresh fruit in the settlement). It actually tasted like apples, but that may have been the trickery of the imagination, or the beer. One particular night Doug and I had way too many of Tim's homebrews. It was time for us to return to the staff house — just one hundred yards directly across what served as the main street. The only problem was there was a major snowstorm with whiteout conditions. But how hard could it be to walk a straight line to the safety of our house? As it turns out, incredibly hard. Your internal compass lies to you when you cannot see where you are going, aided by fuzzy logic. When we realized we were off course, we collapsed on a snowbank, one of many created by the swirls of wind, and laughed at the humour of the situation. Doug wisely roused me out of my stupor and remarked that it was dangerous to stay where we were. If any Ski-Doos came flying over the snowbanks, as young people in search of thrills often did in such conditions, they would land on top of us. We made it back safely.

People "smuggled" booze into the settlement when they arrived by plane, and it was almost a given that anyone visiting Eskimo Point would bring a bottle of something with them. More often than not, the bottle of liquor would be placed in the centre of the living room table and would be drunk in one sitting by various friends who visited the recipient of the gift. Friends had the canny ability of visiting at just the right time, knowing a bottle of the good stuff would be there, and not leaving until the bottle was as empty as the evening. There was one other way to get beer in winter, and that was to drive the Ski-Doo and *kumatik* (sled) north across the snow-covered frozen tundra to Rankin Inlet to the Hudson's Bay store, which was legally allowed to sell beer only. This was not an easy task, as the distance was over two hundred kilometres! But Doug and I would hear the stories of brave souls who made the journey. The financial reward was worth it if the entrepreneurial hunter could avoid the RCMP officer on his way into the settlement. Besides loading up the *kumatik* with cases of Labatt Blue, the hunter also had to make sure that the merchandise didn't freeze on the way back. There was talk that if you drank beer that had been previously frozen, the result was the runs. But, you know what? Beer was so scarce, you did it anyway. All this for a can of Blue!

One night I was sitting in the bath, full with bubbles to disguise the brown water and its smell, with a radio by the side. I would scroll through the tuner, hoping to find music or news, just anything to put me in contact with the outside world. We could usually get CBC Churchill, but that was about it. Sometimes, when atmospheric conditions were right, we could receive Canadian radio stations further afield. This one particular night, as I dialed through the frequency, I picked up, of all things, Radio Luxembourg all the way from Europe. By a freak of conditions its signal was bouncing off the atmosphere, and there I was, languishing in the bath surrounded by smelly bubbles, hearing the latest pop music all the way from Europe.

The Northern Lights were extraordinary. If we were lucky enough to have a relatively clear, cool night, Doug and I would wander to the edge of the settlement and hope to catch a glimpse of this astronomical miracle. Watching them swirling like multicoloured mythical snakes across a black ink sky, you could understand why the aboriginal people thought that they were the sign of a spiritual being. They filled me with wonder the first time I witnessed them; I could only imagine what a Bay boy from three hundred years previously thought of this unique cosmic display. We never tired of seeing them, no matter how many times they magically appeared.

I occasionally visited the homes of teachers to have tea and play chess, and as it turns out they would encourage me to read certain books that they had in their libraries to continue my education. I had never been a great reader of books (my school exam results reflected that), but one of the books that I read had a profound impact on me: *Man's Search for Meaning* by Viktor Frankl, the true story of how the author survived life in the Auschwitz concentration camp, and how that experience led to a greater understanding of life. I believe to this day that that was the book that encouraged me to eventually continue my education.

There was an uneasy alliance between the teachers and the Company. Because the prices in the store (like all northern stores) were exceedingly high, the teachers felt that the Hudson's Bay Company was ripping off their customers. And why wasn't there any fresh produce? I would often have to explain that the price of flying in goods was astronomical. Part of my duties was the ordering and pricing of merchandise, so I was well aware of exactly how much things cost and how much markup the Company made. The example I used was a ten-pound sack of potatoes. Freight charges by the weekly Transair plane were thirty-five cents a pound. So there was $3.50 just for transportation. This was on top of the wholesale price and the profit. So if we ordered potatoes, they sold in the store for about five dollars. In 1973, a ten-pound sack of potatoes sold for about ninety-nine cents down south. If the produce didn't freeze en route, it would spoil quickly in the store, where only the teachers could afford its high price. That was why almost all of the food was in tins and came in via the ship once a year, as the freight charges were remarkably lower via sea than via air. Even today, the outrageous cost of food in the Canadian North is one of the biggest problems for residents.

Ordering dry goods was fun. It was similar to looking in a mail order catalogue and picking anything you wanted, but of course I had to believe they would sell. Individual dry goods (jeans, shirts, gloves, and so on) weighed relatively little, so they could be flown in regularly when we ran out. The order books of each department kept a good record of the history of any particular product: if and when it was ordered, how many, and how much. If something was selling, I just reordered that item and increased the volume. I couldn't order heavy things like nails or tools because the freight cost was too high, unless it was a special order from one of the customers. But I could experiment with some things that were lacking in the store. For me, that was music. So I was able to stock the store with records and eight-tracks that were popular at the time: Deep Purple ("Smoke on the Water"), Chicago ("Feelin' Stronger Every Day"), Cher ("Gypsies, Tramps & Thieves"), and the Carpenters ("Top of the World"). I ordered Motown eight-tracks (Marvin Gaye and the Four Tops) for myself to be played on my new combination eight-track and turntable; those purchases, of course, being signed away on my Company account!

I noticed that the pharmaceutical and beauty supply section, or Q section (really just a couple of shelves), didn't have any nail polish for the girls and women of the settlement, so I ordered about a hundred bottles of various shades, plus bottles of nail polish remover. The day they arrived, I unpacked them, priced them, gave each colour its Q item number, and arranged the small bottles neatly in a row on the centre shelf. By the end of the following day, they were all gone.

I proudly went into Ralph's office and declared my experiment of ordering these goods a retail success. "You fool," he said. "They are not buying the polish to look pretty, but to get high!" In my naïveté I thought the women would enjoy the fashion item (and some did, as it turns out), but the majority were used for sniffing by people of all ages and sexes. This wasn't the only problem the settlement had with substance abuse. I was shocked to discover that some of the young people were getting high by sticking their faces in the open holes of empty forty-five-gallon drums of gasoline and inhaling the fumes. I never ordered nail polish again.

# CHAPTER 8

# Winter

As winter approached the nights became longer and the days much shorter — only three to four hours of sunlight. The snow came thick and fast. The whole settlement prepared for six months of extreme weather.

To pass the time we read Zane Grey cowboy novels and old *Reader's Digest* magazines, and played cribbage and chess. We wrote letters home. A nightly walk through the tiny settlement was our only exercise. There was no point in going much further, as there was nothing beyond the last small matchbox houses except endless tundra and a twelve-foot-high wooden cross marking the settlement's location.

There was a curling rink (not that I knew what that sport was), but the year I was there it was out of commission. The big event of the week was movie night, held in the community hall, followed by a dance. A movie was flown in once a week, provided the plane could land. There weren't any VHS tapes or DVDs back then, so the film was on six individual reels. The lights would go out, there would be a hushed excitement, the single projector would purr to life, and the images would flicker on a small screen mounted on the stage at the front. But every twenty minutes the lights would be turned back on, as the spool had to

The staff house in winter.

The main street leading to the store. The staff house is to the left.

be changed and the projector reloaded. It killed the excitement, but it was a relief to have some form of modern entertainment.

The community's movie was not the only one sent to Eskimo Point. The construction camp at the edge of the settlement also received a motion picture each week. The camp was full of men who worked on various projects, most particularly the building of a new school. They worked twelve-hour days, seven days a week, played bullshit poker with their paycheques, drank whenever bottles of booze could be smuggled in, and were under strict orders not to fraternize with the locals, particularly the women. As such, they existed in their own closed world. Their movie night was also eagerly anticipated. One particular evening at our community centre all the locals were settling in their chairs, ready for the weekly entertainment. The lights went out, the projector started, and the images came on the screen. But this was no family flick. It was *Dagmar's Hot Pants, Inc.*, a soft-core adult movie

The cross was the only marker beyond the settlement.

intended for the men at the camp. But rather than be shocked at the lurid images, the audience howled with laughter, adults and children, as super-curvy women wiggled down the street in high-cut shorts and jiggled enormous naked breasts, and the male actors, watching these exaggerated moves, stared and panted like foolish wolves through their droopy moustaches. Up at the camp the men must have felt deflated with their family feature, possibly *Mary Poppins.*

The dances after the movie were always a fun time. The chairs would be collapsed and the screen raised, and the band would take their place on the small stage. There were a number of talented musicians in Eskimo Point who could play guitars and accordions. Occasionally there was also the traditional drum dance, the drum being an animal skin stretched over a circular frame that is rotated back and forth by the player while being drummed. The drumming would be accompanied by chanting. These dances were also the first time I had a DJ job. My father had been sending over my collection of seven-inch 45s in bunches. The word had got around that I was "the music guy." So one night, I was asked to play records. We hotwired an amplifier to my stereo that I had bought at the Company store, the kind that had not only a turntable but also a built-in eight-track player, a musical medium that was in fashion in the early seventies. I would play one song on the turntable and then switch to the eight-track player for the next song to create a flow of non-stop music. It worked marvellously well, and it may have been the first time many of the Inuit had heard "The Jean Genie" by David Bowie or "All Right Now" by Free or "Brown Sugar" by the Rolling Stones.

One piece of music that I was introduced to while I was in Eskimo Point was the album *Tubular Bells* by Mike Oldfield on Virgin Records. (Having listed my 45 rpm singles back in England alphabetically by label, I had never heard of this label before. No wonder. It was Virgin's very first release.) A teacher had returned from a trip down south with the album and mentioned a new movie everyone was talking about

— *The Exorcist*. He regaled us with stories of patrons passing out in the movie theatre or screaming at the horror scenes. Apparently it was the must-see movie of the year, and the opening piano solo from *Tubular Bells* was used on its soundtrack. We had no idea. As it turns out, the album's success — it went to number one in the U.K. and Canada — established Virgin Records and its visionary founder, Richard Branson, as major players in pop culture.

Storms occasionally lashed Eskimo Point, providing us with unusual, and ghostly, entertainment. We could see the storms approaching from the living room of the staff house, which had a panoramic window looking out to the water; dark, ominous clouds gathering over the vast landscape. If it was an electric event, we could see the bolts of lightning like giants' legs striding toward us from miles away against the backdrop of a purple sky. But ultimately, the only real activities and distractions were doing the chores, preparing our hunting equipment, and going out on the land.

Two hunters building a *kumatik*.

I had to learn to deal with the cold. Snowmobile boots were the store-bought footwear that was most often used when just working or walking around the settlement. However, as we watched the silver mercury slowly descend down the thermometer positioned outside the staff house kitchen window, the dark-blue boots no longer seemed very warm. The sole, plus the rubber tips at toe and heel, could freeze in extreme weather or deep snow, and the cold would cut through the felt lining. The answer was to use what the Inuit used — caribou *kamiks*. These were soft boots made out of caribou skin and fur that reached up to just below the kneecap. On the inside were handmade duffle socks, essentially colourful booties, which acted as a lining. The combination of the two was incredibly warm, comfortable and light. One of the Inuit women came to the door of the staff house one night to tell me I needed her handiwork. She held up *kamiks* and duffle socks that she had already made in anticipation of my realization that snowmobile boots were for tourists. That was the best purchase I made the whole

Hunting out on the land.

time up North. Having frozen feet is a horrible feeling. I also learned to always wear a toque (a word I had never heard before) because, as I was told, 30 percent of heat loss occurs through a hatless head, and to replace gloves with mitts. With fingers apart, body heat isn't trapped. But keeping fingers together in the mitts, like bodies cuddling up to each other in a single sleeping bag, keeps the hands warmer. You needed as much protection, and common sense, as possible whenever you went out on the tundra to hike or hunt.

Caribou, ptarmigan, and Arctic hare were the usual quarry during the winter. One day there was a buzz of conversation amongst the people in the store. I came out of the backroom to see Tim and Louie, the store helpers, drop their boxes and pricing stamps and join a host of other people in running out the door. "What's up?" I asked Doug. "The caribou have arrived," he answered. This was confusing to me. How could people just suddenly quit work and go hunting? It was alien to my Protestant work ethic. But, of course, it was not alien to the Inuit culture. The caribou represented food for many weeks, even months, and its fur would be used for new *kamiks*. To kill one was a family priority. And so we were left with a half-deserted store while the majority of the village went in search of supper.

Ralph and Doug were keen hunters. I had never hunted, and to be honest felt uneasy killing another creature. I had bought a pump-action .22 rifle in the store, but it was more for target practice than anything else. The first time Ralph and Doug took me on the land, I rode in a "skiboose," a passenger sled hitched to the back of a Ski-Doo. I was bundled up against the cold, like a tourist, with a brand new parka, snow boots, gloves, and a blanket. The loud machines roared across the tundra, and I had to keep my face buried in the fur hood of my parka to stop my unprotected cheeks from freezing. After about an hour or so we spotted a herd of caribou and gave chase. They dodged and weaved, and we followed. My hands clutched the sides of the skiboose as Ralph throttled to top speed and we roared across the tundra.

And then I realized that my hands were sweaty and clammy inside my mitts, and yet it was about -20°C. I felt guilty, for I realized I was enjoying this sport. It was a thrill. Ralph then suddenly stopped his machine, quickly grabbed his rifle that was slung over his shoulder, took aim through his telescopic sight, and pulled the trigger. The loud crack of the bullet shattered the silence of the wilderness. Down went a caribou. We made our way to the kill. I felt sad. This majestic animal that only a few seconds ago was running free on the land was now just dead meat.

Doug and Ralph skinned the animal while I watched. We returned to the settlement with enough fresh meat to last us for months. Of course, we didn't need a freezer to store the carcass, just a frozen cupboard padlocked outside the staff house. I soon got over my guilt, and we hunted regularly all winter when the weather was not extreme.

As a novice hunter, one of the first things that you are taught is to be wary of all things metal when out on the land. Metal freezes quickly and can do incredible damage if it comes into contact with naked human skin. One time I forgot to take my watch off. It was

Atop Wolf Esker searching for game.

still on my wrist as I joined my friends hunting. After an hour or so I noticed something was wrong with my lower arm. The metal base and parts of the watch face had frozen and had "burnt" my wrist. The scar took a long time to heal. Another time while out on the land, we had stopped to eat. Someone in the party brought out some Spam, a mainstay of a northern diet. He opened the top of the tin with the key that was supplied with the can, revealing the tip of meat. A large hunting knife was produced, and quickly a chunk of the Spam was sliced off. With the meat speared on the tip of the knife, he raised the food to his mouth. Unfortunately, the blade's temperature was below freezing and it stuck to his lips. He quickly pulled the knife away, but he lost some skin. There was also talk that if your hand was frozen to your Ski-Doo's handlebars (sometimes when attempting to start the engine with a pull of the cord, a naked hand might mistakenly grip the handlebar for extra leverage), you should not attempt to pull the hand away. It would rip all the skin off. Apparently, as the story goes, you are to ask a male friend to urinate on the frozen fist in the hopes that warm pee would free the errant hand. I'm not sure if this is true, or if it even works, but it reminded you of the dangers of frozen metal.

One of the great delights about hunting was the social aspect of it. If you were on the land and spied another individual some distance away, you turned course to join them, regardless of who it was. When the two parties met, a camp was made, a Coleman stove was fired up, a kettle was filled with snow and boiled for tea, and bannock was prepared, then fried in a sizzling pan. You may never have met the man before, but that did not matter. It was the camaraderie of the North. In the relative cozy atmosphere of a less-than-freezing tent, stories were exchanged (or just smiles and hand language was used, if language was a barrier) and talk of the hunt or weather conditions were imparted. To this day I think that is one of the most wonderfully civilized things. It is ironic that in a land where the population is sparse, people go out of their way, literally, to communicate with other humans. Yet in the

A traditional hunter.

A successful hunt — caribou tied to the *kumatik*.

city, where there are millions of souls passing on the street every day, people consider it unusual, even disconcerting, if you say hi to or smile at a stranger.

On Christmas Day, 1973, it was -35°C, and that was before the wind chill factor. A tall, twirly lamp stand decorated with tinsel acted as our holiday tree. There weren't any presents for me or Doug, as the plane, due to bad weather, could not land. However, three local girls, Patsy Kowtak, Nellie Karetak, and her sister Nancy, had given us bibles, thinking it would mend our perceived wicked ways. (Years later, Nellie became the commissioner of Nunavut, and Nancy became a member of Parliament for Nunavut.) Despite Eskimo Point's small size, there were three churches and missionaries, and historically there had always been friction between the Church and the company that had opened up the wilderness to civilization. There was an old joke that HBC didn't stand for Hudson's Bay Company but "Here Before Christ." The traders of furs had arrived in the Arctic wilderness before the traders of souls.

Ralph, as the manager, would host a big Christmas supper. The fat turkey that had remained frozen for months was thawed and prepared along with whatever vegetables were available. With the big bird in the oven, Ralph sought out the bottle of rum that he had saved for the occasion. He then settled on the chesterfield with his small transistor radio and attempted to tune in the Montreal Canadiens hockey game. Reception was poor at best, and Ralph continually manipulated the direction of the radio and the aerial just to receive the faintest of signals. Eventually he grew frustrated and drunk, and fell asleep.

Doug then told me a wonderful story that had happened during one of the previous holidays. One of the clerks (it may have been Doug) had mischievously anticipated a similar situation and prepared a Cornish hen garnished like the big bird in the oven. While Ralph dozed off, he had crept into the house and replaced the fat turkey with its tiny cousin. An hour later Ralph awoke from his nap, rushed to the kitchen to make sure that he hadn't burnt supper, and was shocked to see dinner shrunk to an eighth of its original size. Doug told him what they had done, and how the original bird was cooking in the oven at the staff house. It was an unforgettable story, one that I would repeat for many years. No such practical joke this holiday, but it was my first Christmas in Canada and my first away from home, and as unforgettable as seeing a polar bear in the wild.

Doris and Tim McQuade, the couple opposite the staff house, gave me a puppy for Christmas. Their family dog had had a litter, but they were not sure who the father was. I named the little brown scamp "King," but he was no royal hound. He was full of mischief, tearing up pillows and papers, but he was a wonderful distraction, especially on those long, dark nights in the staff house. While he was still a small puppy, Doug and I would watch him attempt to climb onto the couch where we sat. He would take a running jump, fall short of his target, and then try again. Eventually, he was big enough to make it. His "home" was in the back area off the living room, where he had a comfortable basket and where I placed his food and water dish.

As he grew bigger he would go for walks with me around the settlement, and the local Inuit would smile and chuckle at my *kabloona* ways. Animals, dogs in particular, were not domestic pets to the Inuit. They were working animals. The few hunters who still had dog teams instead of Ski-Doos chained their aggressive animals up outside their small houses. I had to make sure King did not wander too close, or he would be attacked and possibly killed. Doug and I strung up a rope between the roofs of the new and old staff houses. We created a loop leash that allowed King to run the length of the rope, about 50 yards, and remain outside all day while we worked in the store. We also built an outside kennel for him. He was turning into a wonderful dog.

One day, King got very sick. He was so fragile and weary that I had to care for him all night, giving him milk and water. He was close to death. I found a blanket in the cupboard and lined his basket with it to make him more comfortable in what I thought would be his final hours. I felt very sad. The next day at the store, Ralph called me into the office. Mary, the Inuit woman who cleaned our house, had made a complaint. She could not speak English, and Ralph's wife, Jackie, had to translate. As it turns out, the blanket I had chosen to comfort my dog with was a four-point Hudson's Bay blanket — it cost hundreds of dollars even then. It was a prized possession for anyone who owned one. In Mary's mind, there was no way that a sick mongrel puppy should be comforted with an item that was the envy of every Inuit. I had to agree. I hadn't realized. Mary retrieved the blanket and cleaned it. As for King, he came back from the brink of death with one big vomit. The next day, he suddenly coughed up a huge old cob of corn. Apparently, while we had left him on his run he had rummaged through the garbage and had swallowed the whole thing. That would make anybody sick.

# CHAPTER 9

# Spring

Recently, my parents in England made that epic transition from the family home to residential care. While cleaning out the house that had been their residence for over sixty years, I discovered a few letters that I had written to them during the time I worked for the Hudson's Bay Company that they had proudly saved. It was like reading messages in a bottle from someone I vaguely knew; messages that had travelled over the seas of time and had washed ashore as life enters a new phase, for my parents and for me. They provide an uncensored record of a nineteen-year-old full of adventure.

C/o Hudson's Bay Company
Eskimo Point, N.W.T.
Via Fort Churchill, Man.
XOC 0E0 Canada

April 28, 1974

I'm back…. Well, we've been really busy up here. For the past two weeks our Argosy charters [transport planes that bring in supplies by landing on the thick sea ice] have been coming in and we've had to unload the stuff and then find places in the warehouses or store. It's a real pain. The Argosy comes in and everyone dashes down on to the sea ice on skidoos and helps unload the plane (though mostly it's kids; we'd be lost without them). The food and merchandise is then loaded on to *kumatiks* and pulled by skidoo to the store (a distance of about 800 yards). We had about 4,000–5,000 cases of soft drinks. We had to pile most of them in the store as the heated warehouse was full. Talk about crowded, to get into the store you had to buy a case of coke!!!

I had to fly to Churchill (a distance of 150 miles) to go to the dentist. And that was a real experience. While I was there I had to sort out some problems concerning our freight [for weeks, boxes of merchandise had not been delivered], and I was gallivanting all over town with a swollen mouth trying to locate our freight. Trying to describe Churchill to you is

The ice was thick enough for Argosy planes to land on
the frozen waters of Hudson Bay and deliver supplies.

almost impossible, but I suppose the best description would be a modern day Dodge City. Churchill is the last frontier of civilization. The road stops there and so does the railway. There are two Indian reservations nearby and also a large amount of construction workers either passing through or stationed there. But Churchill's biggest claim to fame is the fact that it has two bars, and as soon anyone hits town they go straight to the bar, me included. You wouldn't believe the amounts of fights between Indian, Eskimos, and workers.... There's nothing else to do in Churchill except drink ... it's a drunken orgy, and, of course, everyone is seated. They only stand when they fight. Also while I was there I had to bring back the booze order for the settlement (especially Ralph and Doug) or else I would have been strung up! So I took out two empty suitcases and brought back the booze for everyone....

Yesterday I went out hunting but it turned out to be more of a joy ride. We went about 20 miles and decided to cook something and have tea. We tipped the *kumatiks* on their side covered them with caribou skins to give us shelter so it was very cosy. Two weeks ago Doug, myself, and another guy, Gene, went fishing. We got to the spot with ice holes already dug and an igloo already built. A really beautiful spot and the weather was great, sunny and the temp. about 10 degrees F. So there I was in the classic pose, seated over an ice hole for a couple of hours dangling a rope with a hook on the end. I caught a 2 lb. trout and then about an hour later I pulled out a 6 lb. trout. The biggest fish I'd ever seen on the end of a line. Naturally, I was feeling as pleased as punch! Nobody else caught anything. I gave Gene the 2 lb. trout and we had the 6 pounder that night — nice eating.

I've been here almost seven months now ... and I can now shoot caribou — provided I can hit them. So I've bought myself a .6 mm rifle, a gun with a fair kick and a bloody loud bang! So I've now got that gun for caribou, wolves, and seal. I've also got my pump action .22 (with telescopic sights … flash!) for ptarmigan, rabbit, and for shooting seals while in a canoe. As you've gathered seal hunting is just starting. I can shoot two [the allowed non-aboriginal limit], and maybe if I get two I'll send one [seal skin] home. I could send you any skin as I can buy them from the hunters, but it's fairly expensive. For instance, a wolf skin is worth about $60 (cheap really), but to have it tanned it's sent down to Winnipeg and costs $18 [for the postage]. If you want the head raised with glass eyes and teeth, etc it costs $95, very expensive. Oh well, maybe I'll shoot one.

Last week Doug was out for a week trapping. Some Eskimos asked Doug to go with them on their last trip of the winter to collect the foxes and traps. Of course, he didn't think twice. He really enjoyed himself and came back with some nice stories. He slept in an igloo, which, with the three experienced hunters, was a fantastic memory … the three talking in broken English about past hunting trips and old times. He really enjoyed himself, but lost a lot of weight (he wasn't too keen on raw meat). However, he was disappointed that he didn't come back with a wolf. Doug's due for transfer soon, possibly next month, but he doesn't really want to leave. Wait till our boss in Winnipeg hears that. He'll be surprised. Normally everyone is clamoring to get out of here. Normally a great amount of clerks quit as things are bad. [Just ten years previously, there had been a well-documented tuberculosis epidemic. Two people died, and many were evacuated.] Sometimes this is due to disease, no water, religious brainwashing, and just the lack of hobbies. But as long as you keep up an interest in hunting you don't get too frustrated or mad!

The two parcels of records you sent me arrived … and mom's [gift of a knitted] sweater … snazzy! Ta. I'm just waiting for the remainder of the singles now. I would also appreciate the L.P.'s to be sent before August. I don't think I'll be transferred until September....

Oh well, that seems to be it for now. All the best …

Unbeknownst to us in the North, there was a worldwide campaign at that time to ban seal hunting as inhumane. It was aimed primarily at the Atlantic hunters in Newfoundland and Labrador who killed young white-coated seal pups with clubs. (The Inuit did not hunt white-coated pups or club their prey.) That campaign eventually received huge media attention when Paul and Linda McCartney posed for pictures with young seal pups. Greenpeace embarked on extreme measures in Newfoundland by confronting the hunters on the ice, and also spraying the young pups with a harmless chemical dye, making their soft fur coats worthless. In Eskimo Point, that attitude was alien to the

Skins drying.

84

residents. Seal meat was part of the Inuit diet, and the fur was the main revenue resource for the hunters in springtime. We bought thousands during that period and stored them upstairs in the old warehouse until the ship arrived in late summer. Seal fur was also used to make spring *kamiks*, lighter waterproof boots that replaced the heavier and hotter caribou *kamiks* that were worn in the winter. Warm duffle socks were still worn on the inside. Almost everybody in Eskimo Point wore these comfortable boots at this time of year. I had a pair made for me by one of the local women.

There was great excitement one day when a helicopter landed right outside our staff house. The kids all gathered to greet the stranger. It turned out the lone pilot was on his way further north on some expeditionary business. Eskimo Point was en route, and he needed a place to rest and refuel. As in times past, whenever anyone was in the North for the first time and needed to know something, they went to the Hudson's Bay store. He headed to the office, introduced himself to Ralph, and inquired about a place to stay. Eskimo Point didn't have a hotel, but we had a spare bedroom at the staff house, so Ralph suggested he stay with Doug and me, which he did. We enjoyed the company. It gave us a chance to catch up on news from down south. The next day, by way of repaying us, the pilot took us for a ride in the chopper and gave us a bird's-eye view of the settlement and the surrounding area. It gave me a chance to take some unique pictures. It was the first and last time I was ever in a helicopter.

I had made friends with many of the local families, particularly because I was buying their furs on a regular basis. One of the most successful hunters in Eskimo Point was Simon Kowmuk, and I was invited to join him, his wife, and their teenage son and niece on one of the first seal hunts of the new season. The ice in the bay was beginning to break up. The hunting party would travel to the floe edge. The Ski-Doo pulled the *kumatik*, which carried the canoe, loaded with supplies, lashed to the top.

We stopped occasionally to see if we could spot any seal. Sometimes something that was black and the appropriate length would be spotted a hundred yards or so away. Simon checked as best he could through his binoculars or the rifle's telescopic sight to see what it was. One

Helicopter outside the staff house.

The Hudson's Bay store from the air.

thing that misled hunters was dark garbage bags, either left by uncaring individuals or blown across the tundra by wind. They never disintegrated and would sometimes be frozen into the ice. From a distance, they easily looked like a seal. Once a target was spotted and confirmed, Simon waited quietly by his Ski-Doo, took aim, and pulled the trigger. But even if the shot was accurate, it did not necessarily mean that the end result would be successful. Seals would languish by their air holes, so the trick was to grab the lifeless animal before it slid back down into the black water. Simon was expert at this. He would shoot and then run to his kill in an orchestrated movement. The creature would be skinned immediately, and for this task Simon had a beautifully shiny silver cutlery knife, sharpened to a fine edge and wrapped in blue felt, that he used only for skinning.

We made our way along the floe edge, the pelts mounted inside the canoe, which was still lashed to the *kumatik* and towed by the Ski-Doo by twenty feet of rope. My job was to ride at the back with Simon's son and help navigate the uneven surface by jumping off and pushing either left or right while the sled manoeuvred around chunks of ice. If the Ski-Doo turned right, we pushed the back end to the left so that the nose of the sled followed in line. If the Ski-Doo went left, we pushed to the right. You didn't want to fall over when you jumped off the sled, because the roar of the Ski-Doo drowned out any shouts to stop, and Simon may not have noticed anything was amiss until he looked back, which may have been five minutes or so and half a mile away. It was fun playing a game of sorts during the long journey across nothingness, but it was also dangerous.

And then it happened.

The Ski-Doo had been left on higher ground while we dragged the *kumatik* toward the floe edge. As I was pushing the back end, the ice cracked and opened up beneath me. Down I went. Simon's wife screamed. Luckily I fell in only up to my chest, as I managed to hold on to a piece of broken ice. But was it cold! Once I was back on the firm

Simon Kowmuk with seal.

Skinning the seal.

surface, the ice hole that had momentarily gobbled me up slammed shut. The floes had shifted again. I was incredibly fortunate.

A spring hunting cabin was only one mile away from where we were, so we raced there before hypothermia set in. Once inside, Simon prepared a fire in the old stove and teased me with stories of how in the old days, a hunter would lend his wife to someone like me to keep me warm. I blushed with embarrassment. So did his teenage niece. We all fell asleep.

The second half of this adventure I described in a letter home to England:

At six a.m. some really good Eskimo friends of mine burst in [brothers Solomon and Lewis Voisey]. They're from Whale Cove, a settlement 100 miles of Eskimo Point. They burst in shouting out "It's the Englishmen!" so we sat up drinking coffee and eating bannock until 11 o'clock. We set off then for home, picking up the skidoo and *kumatik* and putting them in one of the two canoes (quite a sight) as the ice had really become bad. We then tried to work our way around the ice. We got trapped at midnight — the ice in front hadn't broken and ice behind had closed up. We were trapped. We couldn't walk as it was too risky. We started to pull the canoe. While doing this the ice started to break around us — the 5 of us ran back and started to pull this heavy canoe before the ice shifted — literally the ice was breaking three feet behind me (I was the last pushing). We had the canoe mounted on the sled to make pushing easier — then the ice gave way at the front and the leader of the party [Solomon] went completely under. He was really lucky. He just managed to get a hand to the *kumatik* which was over his head. He pulled himself up and we all laughed about it — but all realizing that he could have died if the canoe had had momentum to keep going.

We were now completely stranded. The ice was cracking all around us. We found some ice which seemed firm — put up a tent and waited for the ice to break. We sat there just listening to the ice cracking. Suddenly, there was a loud crack, and the ice we wanted to break did so. In the blink of an eye everything was thrown in the canoe and we took off before the ice shifted. We made the floe edge closest to Eskimo Point and once again we had to pull the canoe (the skidoo had broken). That took us two and a half hours and I made it home at 4 o'clock Monday morning — after 32 hours of travelling. I was up at 8 o'clock for work!

Besides all the danger and fun that occurred on this trip, I also saw my first polar bear when I was with Solomon and Lewis Voisey. We were in a canoe paddling alongside the ice when we saw a huge polar bear walking along the floe edge, the unstable margin where solid ice sheets meet open water. Both parties stopped to watch each other. There was a real danger that the bear might become agitated and jump in the water to attack us. We remained silent and drifted by. Luckily, the bear just looked at us for a short while and then turned around and

Trapped on the ice.

plodded away. It was the most incredible feeling to see this powerful animal in its own habitat. No wonder they call polar bears the kings of the North.

The second time I saw a polar bear was far sadder. The only legal way the protected creatures could be hunted was if an aboriginal hunter won an official hunting tag. Only ten were handed out each year in Eskimo Point via a lottery. It was a not only a great thrill for the hunter to win a tag, but it was also financially beneficial. If he could kill a bear, its pelt was worth up to a thousand dollars. Sure enough, one of the Eskimo Point hunters won the lottery, killed a bear, and brought the large white fur into the store and presented it to me for sale. I signalled Ralph to come into the office to oversee such an important purchase. It was terribly sad to see the now-dead creature laid out on the floor like a rug, which is what its destiny most probably was.

The third and final time was far more lively and the most dangerous of all. Eskimo Point lies on the southern migration route the

*Left to right:* Solomon Voisey, Lewis Voisey, and Simon Kowmuk making light of our predicament.

polar bears take in spring to Churchill, Manitoba, which to this day is known as the polar bear capital of the world. I was working in the store when one of the local mothers came running in, shouting about the polar bears. The store emptied of customers in a hurry. I asked what was going on. Somebody explained that the bears would be coming through the settlement, so the children and dogs had to be safeguarded. We closed the store immediately. Doug and I went back to the staff house and waited, watching from a window. The village was deserted. Everyone in Eskimo Point was in their houses. Then we saw the bears come wandering down the centre road. They were looking for food. They tipped over the forty-five-gallon drums that doubled as garbage bins and ripped open the plastic bags, looking for anything to eat. One of them wandered up to our staff house window, looked at us, did nothing, and then continued on its journey south to Churchill with its family, without harming anybody.

Springtime on the ice with Transair agent Thomas Kutlak.

# CHAPTER 10

# Summer Melt

C/o Hudson's Bay Company,
Eskimo Point, N.W.T.
X0C 0E0

July 27, 1974

Dear Family,
I haven't got my transfer yet though it's due in about 4–8 weeks after ship time, so this may be the last letter from me at Eskimo Point. Our ship was due in last Thursday but it's stuck in the ice around Hudson Straits. So it won't be here for another 3 or 4 days and that's when I really start working!! For about 4 days I work from 6 in the morning until midnight unloading the ship. This year we've got 250 tons of freight coming in (nearly all groceries) which is comparatively light. At Rankin Inlet and Baker Lake it's 450 tons!!…

I literally don't know what's going on down south — I haven't read a paper or listened to the radio for a long time.

There've been occasional opportunities to read the Winnipeg papers but I haven't bothered as it doesn't interest me really. I heard recently that West Germany won the World Cup but didn't know the score, and that's the last piece of news I heard....

As for me, things are good. In the store I've got the job of the office, which means I deal with credit and debt, and also buying the fur. Right now I'm buying all seal skin as nothing else is being hunted this time of year. I got this job because Doug got transferred to Baker Lake. His replacement is a guy called Jim from Edinburgh, Scotland.

I was meant to be going caribou and seal hunting last night, but it was delayed till this morning and by then a storm blew up so I'm at home this weekend. But it's not too bad really as I have things to do — write letters, clean my rifles and boots, and clean up the house.... I have also been goose hunting a lot with a shotgun and all together I got three — not bad for a beginner. Really nice eating!...

I think summer's been and gone here — the ice went out on the 2nd of July ... early this year as we had a lot of hot weather, which was the pattern up until a week ago. But for this last week it's been really bad — windy, wet, lightning, but no snow yet. That won't be due till October....

The time in Eskimo Point began to go faster as summer brought the Arctic landscape to life. The days were full of sunshine for about twenty hours. Everything sprang to life. Lemmings dashed through the lichen, geese honked their way overhead, small Arctic flowers bloomed, and the warm temperatures made it a delight to walk for miles across the now-squishy tundra. One of the vivid memories I have is seeing commercial airplanes passing overhead, thousands of miles up in the blue sky, packed with passengers on their way to places like London, Paris, and Madrid. I wondered what they were thinking. Could they see me if they looked out the window, a solitary person in the middle of the wilderness with not another human being in sight for miles? The only things buzzing around me were the mosquitoes — they were everywhere. Sometimes you could see a cloud of them obscure the horizon like a herd of buffalo. I was bitten badly over the eyes, and the swelling made me appear as if I had gone two rounds with Muhammad Ali.

Paul Pemik, one of the young hunters whom I had become friends with, took me out fishing in his canoe. The first time it happened, King, my dog, followed me down to the shoreline. Paul launched the canoe, I scrambled aboard, and we set off. King remained on the shore, barking. He was annoyed that he had been left behind.

Me, out on the land.

"Go back home!" I shouted at him.

But he was having none of it. He jumped into the cold water and bravely swam the fifty yards to the boat, where I hauled him in. He joined us on the trip as we motored at top speed across the water. He proudly and majestically stood at the bow of the canoe.

The warm weather cleared the bay of ice, and the talk in the settlement focused on the annual arrival of the ship and a year's worth of supplies, new gadgets, and the really heavy stuff such as gasoline, Ski-Doos, and all-terrain-vehicles. This was like Christmas in early August, and the season had its own name — "ship time." Ship time was the most important period of the year for any Hudson's Bay employee in the North. Each morning I would gaze out the staff room's panoramic window to see if I could see the ship on the horizon. On the eventful day it was spotted, Eskimo Point was a buzz of excitement and activity.

Once the ship anchored offshore, everyone turned out to help unload the boxes that came in via a rusty, old Second World War barge. It was a tradition for the men of the settlement to help, even though they were not paid. Once we unloaded the barge, we filled it back up with the thousands of furs that we had bought during the previous year that would then be carried out to the ship and loaded on board. There were over five thousand white fox and thousands of seal, plus numerous wolf pelts. At one point one of the barges slipped its moorings and started to drift away. I waded into the cold water quickly, going up to my waist before I managed to grab the rope, and with the help of some of the other workers pulled the barge back to shore. It could have been a fatal move. The captain of the ship, who was standing alongside Ralph, turned to him with a look that implied I was either one overly enthusiastic individual or one brave, but foolish, worker. Ralph just smiled.

We worked day and night to unload and then load as much as we could to send the boat back on its way as quickly as possible. It

Fishing with Paul Pemik.

Fishing camp in spring.

would continue its journey north to other Arctic settlements, hopefully before the ice returned to Hudson Bay. There were almost twenty hours of daylight to help the situation. Exhaustion set in by the time the final barge arrived. We could hardly keep our eyes open, let alone carry boxes of Carnation milk and Campbell's soup up the hill to the warehouses. Ralph made an executive decision and suggested we leave the fully loaded barge tied up at the beach while we all returned to our homes and slept for a couple of hours.

When we returned early that morning, we saw that disaster had struck and the barge had sunk. The rust on the old vessel must have finally given way to the water. A significant portion of the year's food for the settlement was gone. Ralph had to write off a large portion of the yearly order. There were, however, a couple of comical elements to this bad luck affair. Some smart executive in Winnipeg felt it was time the northern stores entered the modern period and had sent up supermarket shopping carts. We had heard they were coming and laughed at the silliness of the whole thing, and now some of those carts were

Ralph surveying the damage after the sinking.

ignominiously sticking out of the water like metal skeletons of some exotic animal. It was as if the ways of the North had had their revenge on the encroachment of modern times. The other was that a couple of the Inuit hunters had diving gear and were in the cold water with their wetsuits and face masks, as if it was a Caribbean resort, searching for bounty. Hundreds of cans of Carnation milk and Campbell's soup washed up on the shore, and families gathered them as if they were gifts from the ocean, which, of course, they were.

By the end of August Ralph told me that the Company was going to send me further north to Coral Harbour on Southampton Island. He felt that in a year or two I would be manager of my own store. This caused me to think. Here I was in Canada, but not in modern Canada. I was in a culture within a culture. I didn't know anything about this place I now called home. And so I told Ralph I was going to quit. A handwritten memo was dispatched to head office, informing them of my decision.

I had been in Eskimo Point almost a year. That September I turned twenty years of age. Some friends invited me over for birthday cake and coffee (and maybe something stronger, if they could find some) to celebrate. As I entered the house, there was a large shout of "Surprise!" from about forty or so people. It was a party in my honour. All the friends that I had made in Eskimo Point, including my Inuit chums, were there. I was choked with happiness. It was the only surprise party I have ever experienced in my life, and one I will never forget.

A couple of days later, and about a week before my departure, one of the local artists and an Anglican minister, Jimmy Muckpah, came into the store. I was in the office. He proudly displayed an exquisite set of five souvenir harpoons that he had created. They were four feet long, with sharpened whale bone at the business end for catching fish and seal, lashed with sinew onto wooden shafts. They were beautiful. He offered them to me at a nominal price. I bought them and still own them today: a powerful symbol of indigenous life, and a constant reminder of my time up North. I will never lose my love and respect for the Inuit.

I sold my guns, and left behind the sheepskin-lined motorcycle boots that I had arrived in, thinking that some future Bay boy would appreciate them. I also left hanging in the closet that dreaded school-boy brown duffle coat, not sure whether it would be of any use to anybody. Whatever unwanted artifact had made its way to the North stayed in the North. As for my black-and-white Fulham football scarf that my mom had knitted for me, I lost that somewhere on the tundra during a hunting trip. I have a picture in my mind of some nomadic Inuit discovering the scarf and wearing it, not knowing he's connected to the London club. That makes me smile.

Besides saying goodbye to my friends, I also had to say goodbye to my dog, King. There was no way I could take him with me. Luckily, one of the new teachers had young children and adopted King. I think he was happy with his new home. Two weeks later I boarded the Transair DC-3 bound for Winnipeg. I had no idea what lay ahead.

Fast-forward forty-two years: Out of the Arctic blue, one of the teenage girls with whom I had been friends with in Eskimo Point, Nellie Karetak, now a middle-aged woman, sent me a Facebook message. I had not heard from her in all that time. She wrote:

Good afternoon dear old friend! I thought of you right away when David Bowie died. You introduced us to him so many years ago which seem like just yesterday … people still talk about you in Arviat. You had an impact.

I was humbled by Nellie's note. But it was also a reminder of how one artist, and maybe one song, can stay with you for a lifetime, and how the individual who had originally turned you on to that tune, that artist, is forever woven into that musical memory, no matter where on this planet you live.

# CHAPTER 11

# Winnipeg

I knew no one and had little cash (my paycheque was waiting for me at Company's head office), and this was long before I had a credit card, so after I landed at the airport I took a cab to the YMCA in downtown Winnipeg. As soon as I walked into the building, dragging a blue trunk that contained my clothes and my record collection, I noticed the overpowering smell of cheap disinfectant. That smell remains with me to this day, wedged deep in my memory. But the place was affordable (about five dollars a day, if I remember correctly), and I secured a room for a month. The clerk told me to stay clear of the top two floors. I could only imagine what went on there.

The next day I collected my accumulated paycheque, and was then richer than I had ever been in my life — even though it was just a couple thousand dollars. I opened a bank account and pondered what I was going to do next. Just being down south — if you can call Winnipeg "south" — was exhilarating. I hadn't seen trees, or shops, or fashionable people for a year. It was enjoyable just to wander around. I had been told that the downtown intersection of Portage and Main was the windiest corner in Canada — and it was. On the side streets, there were lots of displaced First Nations people and ragged young white folks panhandling, playing guitars, and singing for their supper. The two songs they all seemed to perform were Jerry Jeff Walker's "Mr. Bojangles" and Neil Young's "Heart of Gold." And they all appeared to be smoking whacky baccy openly, as if it was a given that this was allowed by the fuzz. I was more than a little surprised with this casual approach. You would have been busted immediately in the U.K.

I started off each morning in an old-fashioned diner close to the YMCA. Each booth had a small individual jukebox, and while I fed myself with bacon, eggs, and coffee, I fed quarters into the machine so that I could catch up on the hits I had missed. There was a cavalcade of dance music waiting for me all at once. I had not heard any of it during my year up North, and then to suddenly be exposed to the musical magic was powerful and enchanting. I bought records in the few cool Winnipeg music shops, adding to my ever-growing collection and knowledge.

The year 1974 had been a turning point for dance music. Building on the Philadelphia sound, a string of hits occurred that demonstrated the growth and power of the genre and the influence of nightlife culture. The first was "Love's Theme" by Love Unlimited Orchestra, written and produced by Barry White. Its luscious arrangement and dreamy atmosphere pointed in the direction that pure disco would eventually take. It's one of the few instrumental tracks ever to achieve number one status on the *Billboard* Hot 100. Shortly after that tune hit the top spot, another predominantly instrumental dance track duplicated the feat: Gamble and Huff's classic "TSOP (The Sound of Philadelphia)" by MFSB, featuring the Three Degrees. But the track that really demonstrated the power and influence of dance clubs was the surprise hit "Rock the Boat" by the Hues Corporation. The song had been released early in the year but was largely ignored by radio. It looked destined for the recycle bin. But New York discos picked up on the tune, and its popularity in the clubs finally persuaded radio programmers to add it to their playlists. It became a monster hit and reached number one on the *Billboard* Hot 100 in July of that year. It was the sound and success of club records that influenced another defining hit of the disco movement: "Rock Your Baby" by George McCrae. It was written by Harry Wayne Casey and Richard Finch of KC and the Sunshine Band, who began to take notice of what was working in dance clubs, as opposed to just reproducing a soul and R&B sound. The single was released on the Miami-based label TK Records. It topped the charts in both the United States and the United Kingdom in the summer of 1974, and would go on to become one of the few singles to sell more than ten million copies. And in September, Barry White achieved his second number one with "Can't Get Enough of Your Love, Babe." This was the month I had arrived in Winnipeg.

It snowed on September 30, 1974. I was surprised to see snow this early this far south. The city lived up to its nickname of Winterpeg.

In those days, if you were unemployed you could visit the government manpower offices. Jobs were listed on cards and pinned to a cork board. It was a sad but useful place. Everybody there had one thing in common — we all needed work. You scanned the board, and if there was a job that was suitable you took your place in the lineup, and when it was your turn you approached one of the clerks, who compared your qualifications with those required by the employer. I saw a listing for a gas pump attendant and junior mechanic for a garage that was close by on Balmoral Avenue. The clerk made the call on my behalf, and I visited the business. Even though I knew little about engines (except my motorbike parts on the breakfast room floor!), the owner was impressed by my year up North with the Hudson's Bay Company. *If they can hire you, I can hire you*, was his approach. I signed on for minimum wage ($2.50 an hour, I believe) and felt slightly stable, anchored by a new job and cash coming in. Each weekday I pumped gas, changed oil and air filters, and installed winter tires on the customers' cars. I was a grease monkey. What was a surprise was to see regular household plugs coming out of the engines. There was no such thing in English cars. The chief mechanic laughed at my inexperience. I learned that when the extreme weather arrived, you had to plug in your car to keep the engine warm. It was crucial to stop the motor from freezing.

There was another young apprentice who worked in the garage. He was the stepson of the chief mechanic. He and I did exactly the same jobs. One day one of the regular customers, a Scotsman, came into the service station as angry as a bull moose in rutting season. Something terrible had happened. His car had been towed to the forecourt. He located the owner in a hurry. The other young chap and I watched from inside the garage as the two men walked out to inspect the vehicle. We wondered what was up. The Scotsman was pointing to his wheels. We could see the owner's face turn ashen. The two of us were called into the office.

As it turns out, the customer had brought his large automobile into the service station to have the winter tires put on. The task had fallen to my young associate. He had successfully changed the tires, but in replacing the wheels on the car he had only hand-tightened the lug nuts. They had not been screwed tight with a lug wrench. The hubcaps were then added, as if the job was complete. The customer had collected his car, paid for the work, and driven off. While going down the highway the wheel had begun to work itself loose, grinding out bigger holes in the rim. Luckily, the man knew something was wrong, pulled over, and called a tow truck. He could have been killed. The owner accepted responsibility and compensated the customer. But there was hell to pay for my young co-worker.

At the diner, I met a guy whom I recognized from the Y. His name was Larry. He was slightly older than me, and his hometown was London, Ontario. He had recently been divorced and decided to shake off the blues of a failed relationship by embarking on a Canadian train odyssey. Larry was funny, upbeat, into soul music, and open to adventure. By coincidence, he had just been hired by The Bay, although this Bay was the big, modern department store on Portage Avenue that dominated downtown Winnipeg. He worked in the shipping department, stacking endless boxes. He was actually trained as an electrician, but was happy for the casual work, even if it was minimum wage. I, too, was now happy for the companionship.

Larry and I rented an apartment on River Avenue. On weekends we would make our meager dollars stretch as far as possible by spending afternoons at an all-you-can-eat restaurant, and at night we frequented Winnipeg's only soul club, The Pool Room in the North Star Inn. It wasn't a discotheque but a show lounge featuring a live band. The musicians wore bright, shiny costumes, had dance routines, and covered the hits of the day. In between sets, a DJ played the big hits, such as "Rock Your Baby" and "Rock the Boat." Larry and I learnt how to do the bump, which was the latest dance craze.

That Thanksgiving Larry and I wanted to do something adventurous, so we decided to hitchhike to a provincial park northwest of Winnipeg. We took limited food and drink and nothing else, anticipating renting a motel room when we got there. I wore my Eskimo Point parka just in case it got cold. Larry had a backpack with extra clothes and a sleeping bag. This was still a period when cars stopped for hitchhikers, so the journey there was no problem. The trouble was, when we arrived almost everything was closed for the season. *What were we going to do?* It was too late to turn back. The only thing that was open was a tavern. We decided the best approach was to get drunk and then crash in the woods. And that's exactly what we did.

It was as dark as a closed closet when we staggered out of the tavern. We walked one hundred yards up the road, turned an immediate right into the woods, found reasonably flat ground, and fell asleep. Larry had his sleeping bag and an extra sweater. I, luckily, had my thick Eskimo Point parka. We survived without being frozen, or eaten by wolves, or attacked by the Sasquatch. In the morning, with nothing open for breakfast or coffee, we hiked down to the highway and hitched a ride back to Winnipeg. Of all things, a young couple who were returning from their honeymoon stopped for us. They were feeling so great with the world, they decided to help out two strangers — us! When we told them how we had spent the night, they were astounded and commented on how lucky we were, as it was not unusual for the temperature at this time of year to drop dramatically to life-threatening status. They drove us all the way into the city.

A couple of weeks later I received word that Pete H., one of the ten who had come across from England with me, had also just quit working for the Company in Red Sucker Lake. He had moved into an apartment just down the road from where we lived. He told us that yet another one of the ten was on his way to Winnipeg. His name was Tim C., and he was still working for the Company. Tim had been posted from the isolated Shamattawa trading post (home of Shamattawa First Nations) in the northern Manitoba bush to an equally isolated First Nations community at Pukatawagan. One night when Pete, Larry, and I were sitting around drinking beer, there was a knock at the door. It was the police. They had brought Tim to the door of my apartment. He had been wandering downtown with an uncased rifle. He had walked into the massive and busy Hudson's Bay department store with the rifle over his shoulder. The police were called. When ordered to drop the weapon, he had started to argue. The gun didn't have a bolt in it, he'd shouted to the cops. He told them that he was there to get the gun fixed, as if he was still up North and walking into a Company trading post with a hunting rifle, which was as natural as buying tea. He was lucky not to have been shot. We explained to the police that Tim was bushed. He was put into our custody for the night with the proviso that Pete put him on the train in the morning for Pukatawagan so that he could continue working for the Company. Things did not work out so well there. Tim returned to England sometime later.

Waiting for the bus at 7:00 a.m. to take you to work in -20°C weather, with snow past your ankles, is not the most pleasurable experience of a working day. So with my newfound wealth, I purchased a faded blue Ford Custom that one of the customers at the gas station wanted to sell. It was a burly beast of an automobile that looked as though it had once been a cop car. The power of its engine was of little concern to me — I was more thrilled that it had a radio that actually worked. I unimaginatively christened her Winnie. Now, no longer dependent on the bus to get me to work, I was able to look for new, higher-paying jobs further afield. I secured a position at a sheet metal factory for five dollars an hour, more than I was getting pumping gas. I had never worked with sheet metal before, but moving from a garage to a factory warehouse seemed logical to the person who hired me.

The factory made aluminum siding for buildings. I was partnered with another young apprentice who had just been hired. We were assigned to a sturdy heavy metal "break," which was about ten feet long. I was at one end, and he was at the other, both of us with metal-tipped leather gloves on to make sure we did not slice or crush our hands. Each morning hundreds of flat pieces of aluminum were stacked by the machine. After we had measured the key points for bending the metal, we would slide the long sheet into the jaws of the break and turn a handle at each end, and the once-plain sheet would be bent into its various required shapes. We did this all day. The only interruptions were at coffee breaks and lunchtime, when a mobile food wagon would pull into the yard and honk its horn loudly, and all the twenty or so workers would stop immediately. The factory would remain silent for the duration.

Despite the monotony of the job, my partner and I tackled the workload with youthful energy, just as I had been taught back in England to perform any assignment speedily, efficiently, and enthusiastically. As it turns out, this was the wrong approach. After the first week or two we were approached by the shop steward and told to slow down. I didn't understand. I thought we were to be praised for our output, but the reverse was true. What I didn't understand was that the union had negotiated with the company owners for a certain amount of days to complete a certain amount of work. The more efficient we were, the fewer days of work were available. We were raising the bar too high. "Slow down; take your time," the shop steward said. To guarantee that we would ease up, we were ordered to take a smoke break every fifteen minutes (I was still smoking then). It was another lesson that I learned in economy. Luckily, the job lasted only a couple of months.

Larry and I didn't have a TV, but we attended the three-dollar double bills at one of the local movie theatres. Three motion pictures are forever locked in my memory from that time. First, a ribald comedy called *The Groove Tube* (a flick that would be labelled as politically incorrect today), which captured the freewheeling, bad-taste humour that was part of a new emerging form of adult entertainment. Chevy Chase was one of the actors, and to some degree its adult satire and spoofing of counterculture laid the groundwork for such TV shows as *Saturday Night Live*, which Chase would later be part of. At the other end of the entertainment spectrum, there was the adventure movie *Jeremiah Johnson*, starring Robert Redford. It's the story of a cowboy who turns his back on nineteenth-century society and goes to live in the snowy mountains, hunts for fur, and ends up crossing paths with aboriginal people. Needless to say, I could identify with the story. There was even a moment in the movie when the Redford character is asked, after a series of tragic episodes, what he is going to do. Jeremiah Johnson replies that he thinks "he'll head up to Canada." The Winnipeg movie audience cheered when they heard that line, as did Larry and I. The other movie memory I carry with me from those days is that of the cult classic *Harold and Maude*. I loved the movie so much that I must have seen it six times since. Starring Ruth Gordon and Bud Cort, it's a black comedy about a privileged teenager who, with no reason to live, continually attempts suicide, but even those numerous life-ending moves are failures. For "fun" he attends stranger's funerals, where he spots someone who has the same pastime — an elderly woman. But she has the opposite outlook — she loves and cherishes life. The teenager falls in love with the elderly lady and, in the process, learns to appreciate life. The soundtrack is by Cat Stevens, and the songs evoke the same feeling as his classic *Tea for the Tillerman* album, such as "If you want to be free, be free ..." Somehow *Harold and Maude* talked to me — an entertaining lesson in how to experience as much as possible, to love what you have, and to always make music part of your life.

Larry, Pete, and I were restless. I had just heard that my brother and his wife in Nova Scotia had become parents for the first time. It was also getting close to Christmas. So we quit our casual jobs and planned to drive to the East Coast to see my brother and his newborn for the holidays — two thousand miles across the continent. I had never driven in ice and snow before.

The night before our departure, two streetwise characters who lived on the floor above us in the River Street apartment approached us with an offer. They had acquired numerous cases of frozen Cornish hens that, as the Brits would say, "had fallen off the back of a lorry." Their living room was stacked with them, floor to ceiling, and melting fast. Did we want to buy a couple of cases? They were cheap. And so we bought three cases (about sixty hens) and cooked the birds in numerous shifts overnight so that we would have food for the road, without having to stop or spend our limited cash. We sublet the apartment to a mutual friend who also looked after the rest of our personal possessions. We filled the car with bags of cooked hens, pickled onions, and doughnuts. (I don't remember why we had pickled onions and doughnuts, but we did.) The trunk was packed with one suitcase each and three milk crates full of my vinyl records. They were more important than extra clothes. We headed south to the border, crossing at Grand Forks, North Dakota, as Larry, being the only Canadian, thought it a good idea to drive south of the Great Lakes in winter.

Our first trouble occurred at the American border. The immigration guards asked for our passports, our business, and our destination. Pete and I had our U.K. documents, but Larry had only his Canadian driver's licence, which in those days was enough to get you across the border. We must have appeared a strange group of individuals: two Englishmen fresh from the Canadian wilderness and a slightly older Canadian, on a carefree journey across North America in the middle of winter. They processed our names through their computers. A couple of minutes later, they asked Larry to step out of the car and come into the office. A guard then asked me to pull the car over to the side of the road so that they could search it. Something big was going on. While the officer started to go through the car, with its bags of cooked Cornish hens, chicken bones, suitcases, and my collection of records, we could see Larry being grilled in the office. The guards found nothing stronger than pickled onions and resonant farts. After about forty-five minutes, they let us go. I think they were disappointed. Not too much to do at the North Dakota border crossing three days before Christmas.

Back on the road, Larry told us what had happened. During his stay at the YMCA, a fellow traveller from Jamaica, whom Larry had befriended, had "borrowed" his passport (unbeknownst to him) to go to Detroit to visit a relative. He naively got as far as the border and proudly pulled out the Canadian passport, but of course his skin tone was dark and Larry's didn't match. Hello! There was now a red flag against Larry's name on immigration records. As for Larry, he had wondered what had happened to his passport. Now he knew. He'd thought he would get around to replacing it when he was heading somewhere exotic, not Grand Forks!

The three of us took shifts: one would drive, one would navigate, and one would sleep. We didn't stop. As each hour went by the bags of Cornish hens became smaller and smaller, as did the supply of pickled onions. The smell in the car was more than ripe, but we were having fun. As we drove through the night and the snow, we continually flipped the dial on the car radio for the elusive local music stations and hopefully some good tunes. We would sing along to such repeated hits as "Lucy in the Sky with Diamonds" by Elton John, "I Can Help" by Billy Swan, and, the most played song of all, "Mandy" by Barry Manilow. We howled the chorus at the top of our lungs like drunken hockey players on a Saturday night binge as the Ford Custom sped through the silent darkness of backwoods America.

During my shift of sleep in the back seat, I was suddenly disturbed by a huge jolt. I awoke groggily to find that Larry had pulled over in the darkness to change drivers, not realizing that a trough, full of fresh snow, ran parallel to the dark road. He had pulled over too far, and now the right side of the car was tilted into a snow-filled ditch. We were stuck in the middle of nowhere. There was not a house, a light, or a car to be seen. It was two o'clock in the morning. As we gunned the engine, the back wheel just spun and spun in the fresh snow. We ventured into the nearby woods and gathered up pine branches, and then wedged them under the tires, hoping to get some traction, but it was no good. We were hopelessly stranded. It was cold, dark, and snowing, and we had only the vaguest idea where we were on the map.

After what seemed like forever we could see the amber flashing lights of a snowplow coming toward us. Relief! We waved down the driver, explained the situation, and asked for help. Could he pull us out? That was against regulations, he said. He then asked us where we were going. Nova Scotia, we told him. He laughed heartily, commented on how crazy we were, got down from his cab, hitched a chain from his vehicle to ours, and pulled us out. We thanked him with as much gratitude as we could muster. "Good luck," he said. "You're going to need it." And then he drove off in the opposite direction.

We were on our way again, but our troubles were not over. I was now driving and noticed that the gas tank was almost empty. We kept going, praying that we would find a gas station still open in the middle of the night. A couple of miles down the road we did find one, isolated and lonely, but it was closed. We pulled in. The worst case scenario was that we would stay there till morning and wait for it to open — provided we were still alive and didn't freeze in our sleep. It appeared the owner of the station lived upstairs. So we knocked on the door of the business as loud as we could. A voice bellowed out from an upstairs window, "Who's there? What do you want?" In thick English accents we told him we were tourists on a driving holiday, working our way to Nova Scotia. It worked. The owner, bless him, came down in his pajamas with his parka on top, opened the pumps, filled the tank, and told us we were crazy. Second time in about an hour that phrase had come up. Maybe we were. We paid him, gave him a big tip, and thanked him very much. We were off again. But our troubles were not over.

By morning we were speeding down the highway, heading into Detroit. Larry was driving. We were making good time, anxious to get to my brother's place by Christmas. There was a turnoff toward the Motor City that we had to negotiate. As we rounded the curve, we hit black ice. The car suddenly started to do multiple three-sixties. We were spinning out of control. We must have done a half-dozen doughnuts. It was terrifying. There was nothing we could do. Luckily, there were few cars about and we came to rest on the highway margin. No damage, except to our nerves. After that we were extremely cautious, not only with our speed, but we also filled up whenever the needle on the gas tank indicator pointed to half full.

We crossed the border back into Canada and made our way to London, Ontario, where we dropped off Larry at his parents' house. After a few hours' sleep and a snack, Pete and I (plus the remaining Cornish hens) were back on the Trans-Canada Highway, bound for the Maritimes. We made it through the confusion of the Montreal road system, the snow of New Brunswick, and eventually to the famous port city of Halifax, Nova Scotia. I remembered that my brother lived about twenty miles along the coast in a place called Boutiliers Point. A number of helpful locals gave us directions, and we made it to the village. There was a Red & White store still open, so we went in and asked if the owners knew my brother. They did! (Oh, the joys of a small community.) And they allowed us to use the phone in the store to call him. He drove up to meet us, and we followed him back to his house. It was Christmas Eve. We had made it. The Cornish hens were almost gone, and the pickled onions had been devoured. The car was smelly. So were we. But we had arrived safely, and it was a thrill to see my brother, his wife, and their newborn at such a wonderful time of the year.

Early in January 1975 we put all our stuff back in the trunk of the car, including my crates of records, and headed back west. The weather was now extremely bad. It was dark. The falling snow hypnotized us, illuminated in the beams of our headlights. The windshield wipers swished back and forth non-stop. At one point the car was not handling well, and I commented that the roads must be icy. There were no other vehicles around, so I stopped in the middle of the road, opened the door to check how bad the conditions were, took one step outside, and landed flat on my back. The road could have doubled as an ice rink. I got back in the driver's seat and proceeded cautiously. We were thankful to eventually get back on the Trans-Canada, which had been salted. There were few cars around (people were being sensible and staying home) but lots of trucks. While we poodled along at a slow speed, the trucks, whose drivers seemed to ignore the conditions, overtook us, and as they did so they sprayed brown slush all over our windshield. You couldn't see anything. The wipers were furiously working at top speed to clear the muck, but for a number of seconds we had no idea what was in front of us. I held on to the steering wheel and prayed there was nothing in front. After driving for twenty hours, we arrived in London, Ontario, to pick up Larry. We spent the night at his parents' house. In the morning, we were back on the road again.

We arrived in Winnipeg in early January, just before an intense winter storm hit the city. You could see the dark clouds gathering on the horizon like a cancerous tumour on an X-ray. We were welcomed to stay at our old apartment by our friend until the storm blew over, and that was a lucky thing because it turned into an event of historic proportions. It snowed for two days, non-stop. The city was shut down. The only vehicles on Portage Avenue were Ski-Doos. It was as if the Arctic had followed me south. We were restricted to the apartment just like I had been in the staff house at Eskimo Point. The rock station on the FM radio broadcast emergency messages for those people who were desperate for medicine or food. Winnie, the car, was frozen solid. It was during this dark period that Pete decided he would rejoin the Hudson's Bay Company. His ninety-day grace period that the company had allowed him was almost up, and as the deadline approached he gave serious thought to his future (unlike Larry and me). After the storm passed and things thawed out, we once again packed Winnie's trunk with the suitcases and the crates of records. With some sadness we said goodbye to Pete, who headed north to Big Trout Lake in northwestern Ontario and a career as a Hudson's Bay manager that would last twenty years. Larry and I drove west across the Prairies to Calgary with the radio on, following the bright, unseen star of adventure.

# CHAPTER 12

# Calgary

Nineteen seventy-five was the mid-point of the decade and, as it turns out, a pivotal year in the history of the twentieth century. It acted as a fulcrum. Things tipped in a new direction, politically, socially, and culturally.

Politically, the year began with a huge black mark on American politics when, on January 1, three aides of disgraced U.S. president Richard Nixon were found guilty of the Watergate break-in. In April, the United States withdrew from Saigon and officially lost the war in Vietnam, a war that had dragged on for over a decade, claimed over fifty thousand lives, and changed America forever. There were two attempts on U.S. president Gerald Ford's life in 1975. And Jimmy Hoffa, leader of the Teamsters Union, disappeared and was presumed murdered. His body has never been recovered. In November, former actor and California governor Ronald Reagan announced his candidacy for the Republican nomination for president. As for Canada, Pierre Trudeau was prime minister, and the biggest talking point was the previous year's Official Language Act, which made French the official language of law in Quebec. Montreal was gearing up for the 1976 Olympics and building a brand new stadium. In the U.K., there had already been a minor revolution when, earlier in the year, the first woman ever to head up the Conservative Party was voted in. Her name? Margaret Thatcher.

Socially, headlines were made on numerous fronts that highlighted issues of gender, race, sexual preference, and aboriginal rights. In the U.K., the Sex Discrimination Act became law in 1975, giving women the same legal rights as men. In the U.S., women were now allowed to join the army, and the first Take Back the Night march was held in Philadelphia. In fact, the strides of progress for women were so enormous that *Time* magazine named all American women as its Person of the Year. In sports, underdog Arthur Ashe won the Wimbledon Gentlemen's Singles title, the first and only black man to achieve that victory, against the swagger of Jimmy Connors. The match was intense, as there was a bitter rivalry between the opponents. It's considered one of the greatest tennis matches of all time. Gay rights made headlines when Staff Sergeant Leonard Matlovich, Vietnam War veteran and recipient of the Purple Heart and Bronze Star, publicly acknowledged being homosexual. His admission generated numerous newspaper articles and put his image on the front cover of *Time* magazine. He was discharged from the U.S. army for being gay, and it became a *cause célèbre* for the LGBT community around the world. Aboriginal issues captured the headlines in the summer of 1975 when two FBI officers as well as a member of the American Indian Movement were shot and killed during a shootout on the Pine Ridge Reservation. Leonard Peltier was extradited from Canada and found guilty of the murder of the FBI agents. He remains in prison to this day.

Culturally, the blockbuster movie of the year was *Jaws*. It was the first movie to gross over one hundred million dollars. And the music that signalled the arrival of the giant killer shark, composed by John Williams, has since become one of the most recognizable pieces of movie music in history. The other big movie was *One Flew Over the Cuckoo's Nest*, starring Jack Nicholson. It won the Academy Award for

Best Picture. Its success also drew attention to mental illness issues as well as the author of the original book, Ken Kesey, one of the colourful pioneers of the 1960s LSD movement. That year, Bob Dylan released *Blood on the Tracks*, considered by many fans and critics to be one of his best albums. It went to number one on *Billboard*'s album chart in the spring of 1975. The new disco sound was beginning to have an influence on the singles chart. In the summer the Bee Gees' comeback single "Jive Talkin'" hit the top of the hit parade in both Canada and the U.S., and the group's reinvention as purveyors of nightclub music pointed the way for their eventual domination with the *Saturday Night Fever* soundtrack. In October 1975, the band Queen released "Bohemian Rhapsody." It became one of the group's most famous and successful songs. It also changed music marketing. The accompanying music video was considered groundbreaking and revolutionary because of its leading-edge special effects. It reinforced the importance of creating innovative music videos as promotional tools to help break hit records, paving the way for the music video revolution of the 1980s. Far more obscure, a little-known group called the Sex Pistols played their first gig in the U.K. in 1975, and in New York a new kind of music and fashion, centred on such clubs as CBGB and Max's Kansas City, was beginning to take form — punk. In Toronto, the iconic CN Tower was finally completed.

But, of course, Larry and I were unaware of any of this that January 1975. None of it had happened yet. We were contained within our blue capsule of reality, Winnie the car, as we travelled across the frozen Canadian prairies, being inextricably drawn west, hoping to find work and more adventure. As the Eddie Kendricks song said, it was important to keep on truckin'. I remember parking the car on the side of the prairie highway the first time we saw the Rocky Mountains in the distance. Larry and I stepped out of the vehicle and stood there in awe of the event. It was a spiritual sight. I took a photograph. It was as if this was the reason we were heading in that direction, as if we had been drawn by the lore of the mountains. With renewed energy and enthusiasm, we got back in the car and continued our journey.

Calgary was a boom town, made fast and loose by oil money. The morning we arrived we secured a furnished apartment on 22nd Avenue SW. We moved in that afternoon. Within an hour there was a knock at the front door. It was the landlord introducing himself to us. He was young, a biker type, and very congenial. "Any problems, give me a shout," he said. "By the way, do you need any grass? I sell it for twenty bucks a lid." We smiled and told him we would let him know if we needed his services. Welcome to the Wild West.

The next day Larry landed an electrician job. I did not have so much luck, but at the end of the week he told me that the company he worked for was desperate for workers, particularly welders. I had no experience, except the sheet metal job, but the company trained me and I became a welder for five months. There were twenty-five workers in the shop, and only four were from Calgary. The rest, like me, were transients or young travellers. The crew was a colourful bunch of characters. My boss was a Brit, originally from London's east end. He was in his late twenties. He had left school at fifteen and apprenticed as a welder, and was full of wild stories of working as a young lad in the factories "back 'ome." One guy who worked alongside me must have been an aspiring math genius, because every time we had to calculate how to bend the metal to a particular shape he would have out his calculator and tape measure, plotting and re-plotting the various measurements. Another chap could have starred in a Cheech and Chong movie. He had long greasy hair, and his arms swung low by his side as he ambled around the factory floor in his blue work coat. He would go missing every thirty minutes to smoke hash in the parking lot. When he returned to work, he would be making small steel hash pipes while he was filling his regular work order. But the most memorable worker there was a woman — Donna. She was short, tough, strong, and the best welder in the shop. She was a single mom with a couple of kids to support. And she helped me out with my welding skills. To encounter a woman in such a grimy and hard job was a surprise for me, but as I look back I realize that this was part of the wave of women's liberation that was occurring at the time. Donna didn't need to burn her bra to prove her strength and independence. She just sparked up her welding rod.

We spent our days in the factory making lighting consoles for television studios. The company had secured a big contract with the Canadian Broadcasting Corporation. Once we had built the cabinets on our side of the plant, they were dispatched to another area where they were painted (to not only look good, but also to hide the crimes of our welding), and then they were wired with all the various electronic components by Larry's team.

Larry and I lived paycheque to paycheque. At night we frequented the two hippest clubs in the city: Lucifer's and the Refinery. (The manager of the Refinery was Lou Blair, later to co-manage the rock band Loverboy). It was still all live bands then, with many of them being influenced by Tower of Power or the Average White Band, who had a worldwide hit at the time with the song "Pick Up the Pieces." The bump was the dance of the moment, and Larry and I, with the moves we had learnt in Winnipeg, became known for our skills. So much so that we began to meet the other diehard music fans and club people, and before long we had gathered a wonderful group of friends who showed us around Calgary and helped us explore the Rockies. Their names were Mary, Bernice, Terry W., and Terry M. We would not have enjoyed our stay in the city without their help and friendship. We went cross-country skiing in the foothills, swimming in the hot springs at Banff while the mountain temperature outside was at the freezing level, and, when the snows melted, canoeing and hiking.

Our friends also gave us an old television for the apartment. Other than the occasional programs watched at other people's houses, I had not sat in front of a television in over eighteen months. There were a couple of shows in particular that became part our evening entertainment. *Happy Days*, starring Ron Howard as Richie Cunningham and Henry Winkler as the Fonz, was easily our most popular viewing, as it was for a whole generation. The show built on the success of the movie *American Graffiti* and its soundtrack — nostalgia for the 1950s. And in a strange kind of way, it resembled our life, albeit a 1970s version. People were dropping over to the apartment and hanging out, spontaneous happenings and events would occur, we would eat at the hamburger restaurants, and there was an overriding sense of fun, all to the soundtrack of the hits of the day, with me playing DJ. There were other TV shows that filled our evenings: *Baretta*, *Kojak*, and *Mork & Mindy* (which starred a young, new actor-comedian named Robin Williams). But ultimately, television played second fiddle to our love of music and nightlife.

There was one girl at the Refinery who was not hard to notice. Besides being attractive, she was the best dancer in the club and incredibly fashionable. Her clothes and her moves were not those of someone from Calgary. No wonder. She had recently moved to the city with her parents and two brothers from Melbourne, Australia. Her name was Lily. We ended up dancing together, and soon became steady dates for each other.

That May, back in England, Fulham FC made it to the FA Cup Final at Wembley Stadium for the first time in their hundred years' existence before a crowd of one hundred thousand fans. Their opponents were their London rivals West Ham. I was elated, and so wished I could have been there for the match. In those days, soccer was rarely broadcast on Canadian television (and, of course, there were no computers). I had to wait a full day to get the results in the Sunday newspapers. I was hoping they would finally secure a trophy in their long but underperforming career. But they lost, as they always did. The final score was 2–0. However, as my friends wrote to tell me, there was a huge party in the area of Craven Cottage. The locals celebrated as if it was a victory. Just getting to the final was an accomplishment in itself. One of my friends, and fellow Fulham supporter, had attended the match and had bought me a program as a souvenir. I could pick it up next time I was in London. England was now on my mind.

By June both Larry and I were getting restless. He wanted to return to Ontario. I, on the other hand, had applied and been admitted to the University of British Columbia in Vancouver. What a pleasant shock that was. The two A-levels that I had, with a bit of luck and last-minute cramming, passed back at Latymer had paid off. Not only had I secured university entrance, but I had also been given six advance credits for the work. I now had a plan. I was to continue my journey west and concentrate on my education. But before I did that, I wanted to return to England to see my parents. It was their thirtieth wedding anniversary, and a big party was planned. However, I wanted my return home to be a surprise, so I did not inform them I was coming. I also wanted to plug into the energy and the music of England that I missed so much. But I had fallen in love with Lily, so I asked if she wanted to come with me. She said yes! She was just eighteen and I was twenty. We had known each other only six weeks. Funds were limited, so I had planned to sell Winnie the car to a guy from the Yukon who worked at the factory, and he was going to drive it up to Whitehorse and sell it for a profit. The money from Winnie's sale would help bankroll both Lily's and my airfares. Unfortunately, the morning of the sale, Lily was driving the car downtown and hit the side of a wall in a parking garage. One door was damaged — nothing too serious, but enough to reduce the price by a couple hundred bucks. But I still had enough cash to put the plan into effect.

And so it was arranged. Larry returned to Ontario. I packed up my records and a few of my other keepsakes, and left them with my former English boss from the factory. The night before our departure to England, we gathered with Mary, Bernice, Terry W., Terry M., and other friends at the Refinery for a magnificent send-off. I think the club staff was also sad to see us go, as we had been a fixture for the past six months. The next morning our friends picked up Lily and me at the apartment and drove us to the airport. We said our farewells; we could not thank them enough for their friendship. Soon Lily and I were on our way to London.

## CHAPTER 13

# England 1975

Heathrow was as busy as a football stadium on game day, even though it was just six o'clock in the morning. We made it through customs and immigration without any hassle. Outside the exit doors a crowd of people anxiously waited for a sight of loved ones. Frantic hands waved in the air, a few signs inscribed with "Welcome Home" were held aloft, and there were squeals of delight and a few tears as family members were greeted. But we just manoeuvred ourselves and our luggage trolley through the crowd. There was no one there to greet us. To ease the final leg of the journey and not subject Lily to her first ride on a London bus (particularly with luggage in tow), I blew the budget and hailed a cab — one of the iconic London high-ceilinged black taxis. It was maybe the first time I had ever taken a London taxi. Those famous taxis rarely travelled to the suburbs; that was mini-cab territory.

It was unseasonably warm, even that early in the morning. The cabbie said that just three weeks before they had actually had snow, the first time in almost a hundred years that the white stuff had fallen this far south in June. Strange weather, indeed, he remarked. The driver did not know the way to Hampton Hill (about twenty miles away) but did know the general area. Get close, I said, and I can direct you, hoping I could remember the route after almost two years away. But you never forget the route home, and we made it there without any problems.

As we turned into the road of my youth, I experienced that unique feeling of returning to the place from which all things began. The familiar street was empty of parked cars, as it always was in those days (unlike now). I instructed the cab driver to pull over outside my parents' house. I paid him fifty pounds, a lot of money in those days, and led Lily down the driveway, each of us carrying our suitcases. I rang the doorbell. It was still very early — about 7:30 — and I knew my parents would be in bed. After a short wait my mother came down the stairs and answered the door wearing her nightgown. With sleepy surprise and delight she shouted out, "It's Kim!" We entered the hallway, and I hugged my mom and introduced her to Lily. My father, on his one good leg (his other injured during his RAF days) hobbled to the top of the upstairs landing. He almost fell down in the excitement. He slipped a few steps but grabbed the wooden banister to steady himself. I felt guilty for surprising them, thinking I could have caused damage to my dad's leg, but it turned out to be okay. He made his way down to the hallway slowly and greeted me. Once again, I introduced Lily. I wished them both a happy anniversary and explained that was the reason we had arrived unannounced.

As always, we retreated to the breakfast room where mom boiled the kettle and spooned in the instant coffee, and we all sat around the kitchen table beside the window that looked out to the large English garden and talked. My parents wanted to hear all the news, and all the stories, and how Lily and I had met, and what our plans were, and how long we were staying, and what was Eskimo Point like, and whether we had enough money, and why we had spent so much money taking a taxi. As forward as ever, my mom asked if we were sleeping together. If so, there was a bed for us; or did she need to make up two separate beds? Such were the changing times. I filled them in as much as I could in that initial surge of excitement, parental love, and concern. I looked around the room. Things were almost exactly as I had left them almost two years before. I'm sure it was even the same tablecloth (washed, of course). I looked over at their kitchen message board, busy with reminders, coupons, and general notices. There, beneath it, was a souvenir tea towel pinned from corner to corner across the bottom of the wooden frame. Pictured on the cloth towel was a map of Canada showing all the Hudson's Bay trading post locations marked with red dots; a map similar to the one I had seen during that very first job interview. My parents had acquired the item on their travels and proudly displayed it in the kitchen so that when visitors came over, they could point to where I was stationed, as if it was still colonial times. I told them they should finally take it down. I was no longer with the the Company. But they knew that.

The big talking point in the family was the large party in the back garden that my parents had planned. My dad had even ordered a marquee tent to house the food and drink and to use as cover should it rain. This kind of celebration was alien to my frugal father, but it was an indicator of the joy and satisfaction he and my mom felt about life in general. All the neighbours were invited, plus old friends from down the years. The family would be together, as my two brothers were due to fly in from North America (their trip was not a surprise, as they had been planning it for some time — nudging me to book my last-minute flight), and my grandmother had travelled up from Eastbourne. The strange weather, as always, was a major topic of conversation, but also the referendum, the first of its kind, in which the people of the United Kingdom were asked to vote about remaining in the European Economic Community. An overwhelming 67 percent said yes. My father was pleased with the result, as he saw closer ties with Europe as the future of the country. And there was a woman who now was in charge of the Conservatives, Mrs. Thatcher; maybe she could give Labour prime minister Harold Wilson a run for his money. That year, the inflation rate was over a staggering 24 percent, the worst figure since 1800, and unemployment was over 1.2 million people. Sobering information.

As part of the English ritual, I took Lily to the local pub, The Windmill, just around the corner from the family home, for a drink. When we entered I could swear the same old regulars were sitting in exactly the same spots in which I had last seen them almost two years ago. A girl I used to date was now the barmaid. That first week Lily and I went sightseeing in London, shopping on King's Road, where we both bought trendy new fashions, and my friends came around to see me and meet Lily. Mick arrived, as well as friends from the Bird's Nest. We all went out clubbing and relived some of the earlier fun times, which felt like ancient history. The following weekend was the anniversary party. It was a wonderful, happy affair. There was dancing. Lily and I demonstrated the bump to the crowd. My father documented the occasion on his movie camera. The weather was glorious, as it would be right through to the end of August.

In July my dad said we could borrow his new Rover car to go travelling, and suggested we head to Scotland. My sister and her friend had a couple of days' work at St. Andrews Golf Club. I could drop them off there, and then Lily and I could head further north and go camping. My parents had an old continental tent (the kind that's seven feet high and is more like an outdoor room than a woodsman's shelter) left over from the early sixties that they could lend us. They hadn't used it in many years but assured me it was all in good working order and easy to assemble. Famous last words.

As we headed north on the M1, the muffler fell off the sleek new Rover. Then the speedometer stopped working. We felt like the journey was jinxed, but we kept going. As we crossed the border into Scotland, it was as if we had entered a new dimension. There was something distinctly different about the air, the landscape, and it wasn't just because of the fog. We made our way to St. Andrews without getting lost too many times, dropped off my sister and her friend, and told them we would be back in two days to pick them up. Lily and I headed further north with no particular destination in mind. Along the way we stopped at ruined castles and churches, and could almost feel the ghosts of ancient times still living in the ruins. Before darkness fell we decided to finish the journey and settled at a campground at a place called Lossiemouth. After securing a site we parked the car and brought out my parents' continental tent. There weren't any directions, and trying to erect the high-standing frame and cover it with the nylon shell was like trying to fold a map into its perfect position. No matter how many different attempts we tried, it never sat properly. In the end, with nighttime almost upon us, we had to settle for the skirt of the tent sitting only as low as six inches off the ground. We stacked suitcases and bags to block off the breeze so that we could at least be comfortable in our sleeping bags. There was a café on-site, so we closed out the day by eating and having a beer with the locals. We met a few members of the RAF at the pub and made polite conversation with them. They told us they were stationed close by. Once they discovered we were from Canada, the inevitable stories of having cousins in Canada began: "Do you know Joe in Regina?"

That night we did not sleep well. Besides the draft coming in, there was what sounded like the constant squeal of birds. And at sunrise we were blasted out of our sleeping bags by the most outrageous noise of jet engines. I ran out of the tent to see what it was. RAF jets were taking off from the field next to the campsite. No wonder we had met the fly boys last night. This was RAF Lossiemouth, one of the main military installations for state-of-the-art warplanes, and they were roaring directly over our heads before we had even rubbed the sleep from our eyes. We had erected our tent at essentially the end of the runway, on the other side of a tall hedge. Once they had passed, Lily also remarked about the constant squeaking noise of "sick birds" during the night. They were not sick, I answered. They were bats. "Yikes!" was her response. That did not go over well. As it turns out, we enjoyed the rest of our time in the area exploring the Scottish countryside, and then returned south, picked up my sister and her friend, and drove back down to London without further incident. My parents laughed at the story when we told them of the various hiccups in our journey.

That August Fulham FC was drawn against archrivals Chelsea in a brand new pre-season competition called the Anglo-Scottish Cup (it lasted only from 1975 to 1981). This gave me a chance not only to see my team but also to take Lily to Craven Cottage and show her first-hand the joys of English football. I asked her if she was comfortable with standing in the cheering section of the Hammersmith End. She was. So that bright, sunny afternoon we stood on the terraces and watched Fulham defeat Chelsea 1–0. But there was that other game going on as well, the fight on the terraces, which the Shed boys were determined to win. It was no contest, really. Chelsea's large contingent of hard core fans had surrounded the much smaller group of loyal Fulham fans. We were completely outnumbered. One particular pint-sized Chelsea individual, who must have had a Napoleon complex, was continually going around instigating fights. When one flared up, he would back away and let the big boys take over. It became so precarious for the Fulham fans that the police corralled us and forced us out of the ground — our home ground! Outside there were problems and we witnessed one Fulham fan being trampled by a marauding group of Chelsea lads. There were dusty boot marks all down his back and across his head, but he was able to stand and the St. John Ambulance people took care of him. Lily was in disbelief at this seemingly normal ritual.

Football hooliganism was so entrenched in the game at this point that newspapers such as the *Daily Mirror* and the *London Evening Standard* published a "League of Violence," denoting which teams had the worst records for arrests and assaults (Manchester United and Chelsea were listed at the top). When the 1975 football season started on August 16, it was marked by extreme acts of violence up and down the country. There were many arrests, and blood was spilt. Knives, darts, and other weapons were used by the warring factions. One newspaper photograph even captured a fan swinging an axe. At Wolverhampton, the visiting Stretford End boys from Manchester United went on a rampage. Fourteen people were stabbed, and shops were looted. The fans were finally subdued with the aid of police on horseback and with dogs. Hooliganism would be named the English disease of the 1970s.

Musically, the two big number one hits that month in the U.K. were "Sailing" by Rod Stewart and a song called "Barbados" by Typically Tropical, which sang the virtues of a Caribbean holiday. I purchased both tunes and packed them in my suitcase with other important items that I had left behind at my childhood home (mostly records). Lily and I returned to the peace and relative normalcy of Canada at the end of the month to begin the next chapter of our new lives. A week after we left, the London Hilton hotel was bombed by IRA terrorists. Two people died and over sixty were injured.

# CHAPTER 14

# The Incident in Vancouver

Returning to Calgary after two months in the centre of the London pop world was a culture shock. In just eight hours Lily and I were transported from King's Road to Stampede Row. Our friends met us at the Calgary airport. Mario, a flamboyant Italian hairdresser and a cousin of our friend Mary, had a beat-up old camper van. He volunteered to drive us to Vancouver. I was surprised and somewhat overwhelmed by his generosity, but then again it was the freewheeling decade. Mary and Bernice said they would join as well, just for the ride. So, after we picked up the remainder of my belongings, including the three milk crates of vinyl records from my friend's storage, we wound our way through the magnificent Rockies toward the West Coast.

We arrived in downtown Vancouver without a problem and crossed the Granville Street Bridge over Burrard Inlet, and were in awe of that famous view of English Bay with mountains in the distance. For some reason Mario thought he was driving in the wrong direction and decided to make a U-turn right there and then. Within seconds we heard the heart-skipping wail of police sirens, and obediently pulled over to the curb. With their hands on their leather gun holsters, two burly cops ordered us out of the van. They questioned the fact that we were from Alberta (they noticed the licence plate) and asked whether we were on a drug run. They searched the cluttered van — checking under seats, pulling my precious records out of their cardboard sleeves without taking care not to get fingerprints on the black vinyl, and riffling through all our belongings while we stood there and watched. One of the officers found a brand new pair of platform shoes that I had bought on that recent trip to London, England. They were the height of fashion, something Elton John might wear during the *Goodbye Yellow Brick Road* performances: six-inch high heels with white stitching around the black base — more of a statement than practical footwear. I had purchased them in the hope I could wear them as stage clothes if I ever found a job in the nightclubs. They were probably the first men's platform shoes the Vancouver cops had ever seen. London fashion hadn't made it that far west yet. "Who owns these?" the cop asked, holding them up. "I do," I replied. The cop laughed, and nodded smugly to his partner. "Really," he said, and smirked, with a mental "uh huh" kind of look. After detaining us for about fifteen minutes, they let us go.

Our next destination was the University of British Columbia campus. I checked in at the student area that listed accommodations. There were not many postings. But I found one for the right price (two hundred dollars a month) in the east end. It was on the other side of town, but it was available. Before our friends returned to Calgary, they drove us in the camper van to a street just off Commercial Drive in the heart of what was then the Italian district. The basement apartment was in an old three-storey house, recently renovated, owned by a Simon Fraser professor. He liked us, and we liked the place. The deal was done. Lily and I moved in, and we said goodbye to our friends, who returned to Calgary. We didn't have any furniture, but managed to purchase the basic necessities. Anxious to kick-start my career in music, I visited Kelly's music store on Hastings Street and purchased a high-end stereo system. The purchase was made possible only with a loan from the

Household Finance Company, which appeared to have as many outlets across Canada as McDonald's. I now joined the ranks of millions of Canadians who had a loan and a credit history. We may not have had sofas and chairs or even a table to eat on, but we had great-sounding music. The clerk at Kelly's included Pink Floyd's *Wish You Were Here* as a free bonus. Albums by this ex-hippie, progressive English rock band were definitely not at the top of my Christmas soul list, but when I played this incredibly well-produced work on our brand new stereo, the sound was amazing, especially the track "Welcome to the Machine," which I played constantly. The song's pulsating bass made you feel like you were inside some huge mechanical apparatus. In its own way it was exactly what future disco was aspiring to: a giant music machine that put the individual inside a controlled industrial environment.

By coincidence, one of my old Latymer classmates, Jerry, had moved to Vancouver with his family. I managed to track down his phone number, and while Lily and I were walking in the magnificent Stanley Park one day, I called him unannounced from a pay phone. Needless to say he was surprised, but thrilled, to hear from me. Jerry not only supplied us with a couple of chairs and a coffee table to add to our sparse apartment, but, because he was a manager for the Royal Bank, he also set me up with a bank account.

It was with great pleasure that we discovered the magnificence of Vancouver. Lily and I explored the city, its beaches, the seawall around Stanley Park, and the mountains in the distance. Vancouver was in a transitional stage then, and it was almost unknown to the rest of the world. There were still remnants of hippie and bohemian culture, especially along West 4th Avenue. There were funky record shops, second-hand bookstores, health food stores (before they became corporate), and even artisans who made tooled leather goods. A new radical environmental group called Greenpeace had an office on that street. I had even heard stories on campus that some students who could not find accommodation lived temporarily at Wreck Beach, at the edge of campus, which was well-known as a nudist beach. There was an old gun turret down there where people squatted. But we were lucky and had found somewhere that suited our needs, even if I had to take a one-hour ride across town on the 14 Hastings bus to UBC. That ride along Hastings Street was a journey through the extremes of Vancouver.

I boarded the bus in the Italian district in the east end, close by Baceda's sprawling nightclub that anchored the Commercial Drive and Hastings corner, which featured such artists as James Brown and Ike and Tina Turner. Being that close to the start of the bus's journey, I usually managed to find a seat before it became crowded with students and other passengers who were emblematic of the various neighbour-hoods the bus travelled through. Before it reached the heart of the city, it ran along the lower east side, past the doss-houses and the cheap but famous The Only seafood restaurant (which still had sawdust on its floor, like in an old Wild West saloon, that trailed out onto the side-walk), across Pigeon Park, where the homeless and addicted souls congregated, and past Woodward's department store and the huge Save On Meats, with its busy shoppers. And then the bus turned left onto Granville Mall, with its uptown shops, including the Hudson's Bay department store, past the numerous head boutiques that sold pipes and rolling papers, with homeless youth hanging out in the doorway, either selling dope or scrounging it. Then past the sex shops, as the 14 Hastings crossed Davie Street, skirting the multitude of high-rises that stood shoulder to shoulder in the densely populated West End, along busy Broadway, and then slowly up the West 10th Avenue hill, with its fashionable and expensive houses. And then the bus raced through the extensive woodlands (where no one needed to get on or off) that surrounded the campus, finally terminating in the heart of the campus, close to the Student Union Building. The many young passengers whom the bus had picked up en route would then disem-bark in an orderly fashion and join the throngs of students streaming in all directions. There were thirty thousand students registered at UBC, so the pedestrian traffic first thing in the morning and in late afternoon was similar to that of game day at a stadium. New students needed a map to get around the huge campus in the beginning. I know I did. My usual first destination in the morning was the giant cafeteria for a coffee and one of the kitchen's excellent cinnamon buns, as I plotted my day's worth of studies.

Back at our new basement home, a couple named Floyd and Carol lived immediately above us. Unlike the rest of the tenants in the house, they were not students. We didn't know what they did for a living, but they did drink beer with regularity at the Blue Horizon Hotel. We had a feeling that Floyd was a drug dealer. He had the look of a streetwise hustler. She had an eight-year-old son from a previous relationship who, sadly, would come home from school and be locked out, sometimes in the rain. On more than one occasion we found him sheltering under the back stairs to keep dry. So we always invited him in until his mom came home.

As always, we had extremely limited funds. One weekend we did our weekly shopping at a local store on Commercial Drive, spending our last thirty dollars on groceries. The food was placed in two large cardboard boxes. The owner of the store volunteered one of his staff to deliver the groceries, as the boxes were too big to carry. We said thanks and were told that the order would be there within an hour or two. Lily and I did not return to the apartment till late afternoon. We expected to see the delivery left by our basement back door, but there was nothing there. I went to the store, and the owner confirmed that the order had been delivered and left by the door as no one was home. The groceries had been stolen. We had our suspicions about who might have taken our food but could prove nothing. There was no more money to buy extra food till I got paid at my weekend job as a sales clerk at the Bootlegger jean store. We made what little we had last for as long as possible.

For some reason Floyd went out of his way to befriend us, unlike the other tenants in the house, who gave him a wide berth. He said he liked the music that drifted from our place into his living room. "It's not too loud?" I asked him, worried. "No problem," he said. One day he came by to thank us for looking after the boy and, in appreciation, handed us a six-pack of beer. He then noticed the platform shoes standing in the corner like a work of pop art. "Wow! What are those?" he asked. I explained that I had just bought them in England. "Do you walk in them, or do you stand and make a speech?" he asked, and laughed at his own joke. He held one shoe up in admiration. "Cool. Now that's a commitment!" He then changed the subject and mentioned that it was Carol's birthday in a week and asked if we could look after a small present till then so that she wouldn't find it before the big day. Foolishly, I said yes. From inside his jacket he pulled out a small package wrapped in bright red paper. It was about the size of a giant box of matches that my mother used to buy and keep handy by the gas stove. I put it in the top drawer of a desk that we had recently acquired and told him it would be safe there.

A few days later, at about three o'clock in the morning, we were startled awake by the sound of gunfire. "What's that?" Lily said. I had no idea but hoped it would go away, whatever it was. "Go back to sleep," I foolishly replied. Within minutes the police had arrived. We could see their heavy boots and the paws of their German shepherd dogs as they marched by the basement windows. Yellow flashlight beams pointed the way. There was an assertive rap at the basement door. It was a policeman, so, half asleep, we invited him into the small, bare apartment. He told us that someone had tried to kill Floyd. The gunman had waited in a car parked in the back alley until Floyd went into the bathroom. When he turned on the light, the gunman had fired. The bullet had travelled along Floyd's cheek and taken off half his ear, but he hadn't died. They had rushed him to hospital. The policeman asked us if we knew of any strange happenings or any other relevant information that might help. We explained that we had just arrived in Vancouver and knew nothing. At that moment the cop became relaxed and leaned against the desk where the package was stored. In fact, he was almost sitting on top of it. We didn't want to say anything. It wasn't ours, we didn't know what was in it, and it might cause problems. He asked us our ages. Twenty and eighteen, we told him. "You look much younger," he commented, and he wondered if we were underage runaways. No, we explained, just young lovers. He pencilled our personal details in his notebook, told us to be careful, and left.

Floyd returned from the hospital a few days later. He visited us, which was disconcerting. He wanted to know if we still had "Carol's present," so I took it out of the top drawer and gave it to him. He offered no explanation as to what had happened but said he, Carol, and the boy were going to stay away from the house for a couple of weeks. Good idea. So if we heard any noise coming from the floor above, we should call the police, he added. Sure enough, the following day we heard his floorboards being pried open with what sounded like a crowbar. Somebody was looking for something. We were worried. I went around the front of the house, and nervously I attempted to peer in the windows. Yes, there was somebody there. I ran back to the basement, called the police, explained the situation, and waited behind our locked door. By the time the cops arrived, the intruder had fled. We decided it was time for us to leave as well. Our landlord understood, and within a week we had a new apartment on Broadway.

Disco was just becoming popular in Vancouver at this time. It was cheaper, and more predictable, to install a sound system and a DJ than hire a band that required accommodations and countless beers. And there was always the potential for a musical meltdown by a group of aspiring musical heroes on any particular night. So for club owners and managers, it was a no-brainer — constant music with predictability, cheap labour, and no band egos. Needless to say, the change did not go over well with the fraternity of musicians or the boozy pub crowd, but for the uptown cocktail contingent, with their platform shoes, tailored suits, and salon-styled haircuts, it was warmly embraced.

Almost the first thing I did after registering at university and confirming my classes was to become a member of the student radio station, CITR. The station broadcast only to the student union building and the campus residences, but that made no difference. It was a crash course in how to be a DJ. Some weeks later, word went out amongst the radio station team that a new company, Tritone, had cornered the market on disco installations in nightclubs and it was looking for DJs. I had the job in Bootleggers on the weekends, but I needed something more to help pay the rent and my way through school. Besides, it was a chance to become a "real" DJ. I applied for the position and was incredibly excited to be accepted, or at least added to the list of potential candidates.

My first gig was an offer to fill in for one night at a pub that had recently replaced live acts with a DJ — The Port Moody Inn in the Vancouver suburbs. Being so far out of the city, it was impossible to get to by public transport, so I thought I might have to pass on the opportunity. But my old school friend Jerry, hearing of my dilemma, lent me his stylish 1973 Firebird for the night. Well, at least I would arrive with impressive wheels. I wore my equally impressive platform shoes. In retrospect, that may have been a mistake. The Port Moody Inn was an establishment where the waiters still worked the room with trays held high, loaded with glasses of draft beer that sold for fifty cents. The servers had chrome metal units filled with quarters belted around their waists, and they dispensed change like bus conductors issuing tickets. Full-to-the-brim glasses of beer traded places with the accumulated empties that crowded the sticky, laminated tables. As for the music, the patrons wanted more J. Geils Band than George McCrae. Needless to say, I did not get the job.

My next audition was for Ken Stauffer. Mr. Stauffer was one of the most respected club owners in Vancouver. He had owned The Cave

Supper Club, a legendary venue that had resided in the heart of downtown on Hornby Street since 1937. Its decor was almost that old as well. Pseudo stalactites, sprinkled with glitter, hung down from the high ceiling. Mr. Stauffer, who was a wonderful man, had a new modern venture slightly out of the downtown core at the corner of Broadway and Granville — originally called Lula-Belle's, it was now renamed Clementine's and the emphasis was on being a neighbourhood disco and eatery, and nothing grander than that. I got the job.

In those early days the DJ's style was still very basic — they'd cue seven-inch singles using the slip mat, and then mix from one record to another with only the vaguest knowledge of their tempos, just with the basic understanding that the next song was slightly faster than the previous one, or they'd play a slower song if they wanted to cool down the crowd. I modelled my style on those DJs I saw back in my hometown of London. I chose an opening song that became my signature tune, "The Love I Lost" by Harold Melvin & the Blue Notes, not because of its lyrics, but because its forty-five second instrumental intro allowed me to talk over the music, to introduce myself, welcome the patrons to a night of great music, and encourage them to get up and dance. It was, as they say these days, very old skool. Just before the first vocal by lead singer Teddy Pendergrass started, I would stop talking ("hitting the post," as they say in radio DJ talk) and then proceed to dance to the tune in the confines of my DJ booth. It seems hokey talking about it now, but it did the trick, and more often than not my exuberance would entice the first couple to take the floor — and that was usually all you needed to get the party started.

One Friday night, after I had completed my set and everyone was leaving the club, I was approached by a late straggler. "Hi there, music man. How you doing?" It was Floyd. The scar across his cheek had healed and half his ear was missing, but he was smiling. "Great music tonight, but I'd rather hear more Doobie Brothers than that KC and the Sunshine crap," he said jokingly. "You're good, though." I thanked him and asked after Carol and the boy. He said they were fine, and invited me back to the house on Commercial Drive for a beer and something stronger. He winked. It was late, past two o'clock in the morning, so I told him I had to go. It had been a long day, what with classes and the job.

"No problem," he said. "I'll be back to visit you again. I always loved your music."

I picked up my red box of seven-inch 45s and strode away in those fancy platform shoes, careful not to look back or fall over my feet.

# CHAPTER 15

# DJ Skills

In 1975 the most popular record that had songs mixed seamlessly into each other was Gloria Gaynor's *Never Can Say Goodbye* album, which featured three songs in a constant flow. It gave the DJ a chance to take a bathroom break, or get a beer from the bar, while the patrons remained on the dance floor. The idea for that medley came from producer Tom Moulton, and Moulton's remixes would later go on to have a huge impact on disco music. It was Moulton who invented the twelve-inch single — the extended, remixed single-track song that later became the defining tool of the modern disco DJ. The only other record at the time in the music arsenal to allow such freedom for the DJ was the LP for KC and the Sunshine Band. The two big hits "That's the Way (I Like It)" and "Get Down Tonight" were not mixed together, but there was only a one-second break between the songs — short enough to seduce the dancers to stay on the floor. And that, of course, is the trick of every DJ — to keep the people dancing.

It was Mr. Stauffer's connection with The Cave nightclub that gave me my first high-profile gig. Gloria Gaynor was booked to play the venue, and I was asked to be the opening act. My nerves almost got the better of me as I spent the fifteen minutes before showtime in the venue bathroom, but I kept my chops and my bowels together long enough to do the gig and get the sold-out crowd dancing for Ms. Gaynor. It was a turning point in my career, and for the viability of disco as a musical genre. Disco artists could not only have dance floor hits, but could sell concert tickets as well. Or at least some of them could. The argument that the genre didn't produce any legitimate stars would burden disco throughout its musical reign.

The year 1975 was crucial for the genre that came to be known as "disco music." There was the hit "Get Dancin'" by Disco Tex and the Sex-O-lettes. Gwen McCrae (wife of George McCrae) released "Rockin' Chair," a song that duplicated the sound and style of her husband's hit track. It cracked the top ten on the *Billboard* charts and made top spot on the soul charts. The Bee Gees, who had once been a pop-rock group with such ballads as "How Can You Mend a Broken Heart" and "I Started a Joke," now found themselves as a dance music band under the production direction of Arif Mardin. They released the single "Jive Talkin'," which set them on the path to dance music success. Van McCoy's "The Hustle" had club-goers taking up a new form of line dancing. And a surefire floor-packer was "Lady Marmalade" by Labelle, with its naughty French chorus "*Voulez-vous coucher avec moi (ce soir)?*" But the defining disco release of 1975 was that Gloria Gaynor album *Never Can Say Goodbye*, with its nineteen-minute Tom Moulton–mixed medley.

One of the things I had learnt from watching the DJs back in London was the ability to create a medley using just thirty seconds of classic hits, beginning with "Rock Around the Clock" by Bill Haley and His Comets, switching to such songs as "The Twist" by Chubby Checker, and ending up with a current hit such as "It Only Takes a Minute" by Tavares. It required good slip-cue skills to slam one seven-inch single into another without missing a beat, at just the right moment to produce a seamless historical flow, and the perfect choice of song to build the excitement on the dance floor. If done right, it became the highlight of the night, lasting about ten minutes and driving the crowd into a frenzy. It became a signature move for me. Essentially this was mixing before I really knew what mixing was. The idea of the musical medley featuring snippets of songs was also slightly ahead of the learning curve, as the concept would be duplicated in 1977 by Shalamar and their musical montage "Uptown Festival," and later, in the 1980s, by Jive Bunny.

My fellow students from university would also turn up to hear me DJ, particularly those from, of all things, my French course. One of the prerequisites for obtaining an arts degree was to have passed French 100 (or higher). Given my outrageously inept French skills as a schoolboy, I was dreading the course, but if I wanted my degree I had to take it. Luckily, the UBC professor was a delightful and high-spirited young woman from Paris who informed us during the first class that she would make sure that we all passed the course. There were about fifteen of us from various backgrounds and, as it turned out, various ages. One of the individuals enrolled was a mature student — a mom twice our age who had decided to go back to school for the fun of it. Her name was Noelle Vogel. Over the coming months we all got to know each other. In fact, it was the friendliest course I was enrolled in. That was because our instructor made the lessons fun and interesting, including holding classes in different locations such as her house, or outside when the weather allowed, or at a French café. And sometimes, for fun, some students would come for a beer at Clementine's.

Noelle, through the gossip of the younger students, discovered that I was an aspiring DJ. One day she came to class with a gift for me. Her husband, in partnership with his brother, had just started up a record label, and she wanted me to have a copy of their first release. I was thrilled. It was my first promo copy of my budding career. As it turns out, the album became incredibly famous and a big seller. It was *Dreamboat Annie* by Heart. Heart, originally from Seattle, was based at the time in Vancouver. They had developed into a top draw on the Vancouver cabaret circuit, playing such clubs as the Birdcage and Starvin' Marvins. The new label they were signed to was Mushroom Records. *Dreamboat Annie* would go on to become a million-seller and crack *Billboard*'s top ten. The album was recorded at Can-Base Studios on West Sixth Avenue, which later worked out an arrangement with the label and was renamed Mushroom Studios. Years later when I was managing the Vancouver electronic band Images In Vogue, the group recorded hundreds of hours of music at Mushroom Studios. I would even eventually record there myself — my spoken word projects. Today when I hear such songs as "Magic Man" and "Crazy on You" from that album, I'm whisked back in my mind to the start of my career.

I was enjoying university. It was a wonderful counter life to the hedonism of nightclubs, which I, of course, also enjoyed. My thoughts toward education had changed dramatically. Instead of the belief that I once had as a schoolboy that classes were boring and a waste of time, I now had the opposite view. I came to the conclusion, through my own stupidity, that education was wasted on the young (well, on me, at least). I wanted to learn more. After having lived with the Inuit for a year, and then travelling carefree for another year, I had a thirst for knowledge and understanding. Maybe I hoped to answer those big life questions that we all ask ourselves at some point. Why are we here? Why's the sky blue? How deep is a bucket of shit? It was the English 100 course that had the most dramatic effect upon me at that time. Literature was answering the questions I was asking. (That bucket is as deep as you want it to be, I discovered.) After having turned my back on reading books during my teen years, I had to suddenly make up for lost time. I read with enthusiasm such novels as D.H. Lawrence's *Sons and Lovers*, J.D. Salinger's *The Catcher in the Rye*, Robertson Davies's *Fifth Business*, and John Irving's *The World According to Garp*. The young professor I had, an American woman who was also a novelist, encouraged my writing. That first year at university changed my outlook forever. At the same time, my success at Clementine's showed me that DJing was something that I was good at. With relative confidence and financial comfort in our lives, Lily and I decided to do something dramatic. We would get married.

# CHAPTER 16

# The Wedding

The wedding took place in Calgary over the May long weekend, just a month after I completed my first year at university. It was an unforgettable experience ... for all the wrong reasons.

There were over a hundred and fifty people invited to the wedding, predominately from Lily's side of the family. My mother and sister flew in from England, and my brother from Nova Scotia. Our Calgary friends made up the wedding party: Terry W. was the best man, Mary and Bernice were two of the bridesmaids, and Terry M. was the usher. Given Lily's Serbian background, it was an Orthodox wedding. There wasn't a Serbian Orthodox church in Calgary, so it was to take place in a Greek Orthodox church. Lily's father organized a Serbian priest to be flown in especially to conduct the service. Three days before the ceremony, my future father-in-law asked me to join him on a trip to one of the farms on the outskirts of the city. It was owned by one of his Serbian friends. We were going to purchase the meat for the huge feast that was planned for the reception. When we arrived at the farm, we were escorted into one of the barns, where there were a dozen or so large fat pigs snorting away in a pen, something I had not anticipated.

"Which one do you want?" he asked me.

"What?" I replied.

"Choose one," he said.

I now understood that we were killing the beast for our celebration. Sadly, I pointed to one unlucky animal.

"Good. Okay, here you go," he said, and handed me a large sharp knife.

"What? You want me to kill it?" I couldn't do it. I had seen enough dead animals up North.

He laughed, understanding my squeamishness, and took back the knife. I walked outside. Five minutes later I was called back into the barn. The now-dead creature was strung up from the rafters. Blood from the gaping neck wound was dripping onto the ground. I heard the *pop* of a blowtorch being ignited. The blue flame spat out like the devil's tongue. Carefully, it was handed to me, and I was instructed to burn away the fine, coarse hair. That I did, knowing I had to contribute, but I felt sad as I scorched the thick hide and scraped away the char-coaled skin. We loaded the carcass into the van and then drove back to the city.

It was an unusually hot week, and the run-up to the festivities was a three-day party with lots of drinking and eating, and the silliness that always seems to happen on these occasions. Three of the guests ended up in jail overnight for being too drunk while wandering the streets, but somebody managed to bail them out in time for the ceremony. The wedding day weather was sunny and extremely hot, over 27°C. The church was as stuffy as a forgotten aunt's closet. The top hats and tails I had chosen for myself and the two Terrys were not the most practical of clothes to have picked for such weather. Lily was late (as the bride always is), and we waited in the church anxious to get the proceedings started. She looked spectacular in her white flowing wedding dress when she and her father arrived. Being an Orthodox ceremony, there were some unusual rituals that had to occur in a spe-cific series. The first of them concerned both of us holding oversized incense candles that smouldered thick smoke and fumes as we stood at the altar. The next concerned literally "tying the knot" — a silk sash loosely bound our clasped hands. The next ritual concerned walking around the altar three times. However, before that happened, something else occurred. I fainted. My father-in-law caught me before I hit the ground, and along with Lily's uncle, carried me back down the aisle and out of the church. The guests looked on with bewilderment. Outside, the hot air smacked me in the face and I threw up on the church porch.

After discarding my smart tie, loosening the top button on my starched white shirt, and stabilizing my thoughts, we walked back into the church to continue the service. The priest, who appeared to have been indulging in the red wine, was chatting up the bridesmaids. Once things were in place and I was standing with confidence, we tried again. The necessary words were spoken solemnly, and with our wrists once again loosely tied we walked slowly around the altar once, twice … and then I passed out a second time. Back down the aisle I went. More vomit on the church steps. Once again, back to the altar.

The priest now did not bother attempting the third journey around the cross. But there was one more ritual to perform. Crowns were placed on our heads. Somebody put a gentle hand on mine to make sure it wouldn't go crashing to the ground in case I did. Anxious to get the whole affair over with, the priest just said, "You are man and wife." And it was done. We were married.

Some of the wedding photographs included the embarrassing shots of me being carried out of the church, my face as white as Lily's dress. For some reason, I kept those photos.

But the fun did not stop there.

When we arrived at the reception hall, the party was in full swing. The large room, which had been beautifully decorated with paper chains strung across the ceiling, was not air-conditioned. It was incredibly hot. There was endless food and drink. The barbecue pork was especially delicious. The chefs entered the room with the cooked pig's head, now bronzed and stuffed with an apple in its mouth, displayed on a tray. They presented it to my best man, Terry. Diplomatically, he accepted the honour with polite gratitude but looked at Lily and me with a "What do I do with this?" face. Slivovitz, the Serbian national drink, flowed continually. It's the liquid equivalent of swallowing a bush fire. Our guests were getting sauced. There was dancing and laughter. The large three-tiered wedding cake was brought to the main table for cutting. Unfortunately, the heat in the room caused the icing to soften, and the pillars that held up the top two tiers collapsed. The bride and groom figurines toppled onto the floor like I had at the church. Not to worry, we still managed to give everyone a piece of cake. And then the paper chains came unglued from the ceiling and fell across the tables, into the food. We all just laughed at the silliness of it all.

Our honeymoon destination was just an hour and a half away — the famous Chateau Lake Louise in the Rockies. After changing out of our wedding clothes and into something more comfortable, shorts and T-shirts, we drove through the night and into the heart of the mountains, arriving well after midnight. As soon as we stepped out of the car, we felt the bite of the cold. It was freezing. There was still snow on the peaks, and we had not packed anything warm. *Never mind; let's just get to our room,* was my only thought. The night clerk checked us in, congratulated us on our wedding, and gave us directions to our room. Thoughtfully, a bottle of champagne on ice, courtesy of the manager, was waiting for us beside the bed. A nice touch. The room, old but well appointed, was huge and looked out on the spectacular mountains. While Lily was getting ready for our honeymoon night, I decided to explore the room, as you often do in hotels. I checked the desk drawers: Gideons Bible and writing paper. Doors opened into a huge walk-in closet with an ironing board and iron. There was a beautiful bathroom with posh toiletries. And then there was one other door beside the front door that I went over and opened.

"Hey, what the hell are you doing?" said a strange voice.

There in front of me on the floor were three bodies in sleeping bags. "What the fuck?" I shouted angrily. And quickly shut the door.

I went to lock it, but, being an old-fashioned wooden door, there was no lock. Just a keyhole. It could be secured only by a key. I called down to the night clerk immediately. As it turns out, there was a little passageway to an adjoining room, and these were ski bums. The remainder of their friends were in the other room. I asked the clerk to come up and lock the adjoining door immediately. This was, after all, our honeymoon night. He apologized but said that he did not have the master key, and it would have to wait till morning. Ugh! I grabbed the desk chair and wedged it under the doorknob. It would prevent anyone from entering the room via that door. But strangers in sleeping bags ended up sleeping just ten feet away from our marital bed with their ears to the ground on our honeymoon night.

It was a pleasurable couple of days at Lake Louise, even though we had not packed the appropriate clothes for hiking in the cold weather. We spoilt ourselves with the hotel's fine food, and to this day the dish coquilles Saint-Jacques reminds me of the famous hotel and our honeymoon days. Our friends drove my mother up to visit us before she returned to England. When we returned to Calgary, she was in the front seat of the car, sitting between Lily and me on the long bench seat. We had a number of people pointing at us and laughing as we drove back into town. We wondered why, and then realized that the "Just Married" graffiti was still on the car. We must have looked a comical sight: a newly married couple with the mother sitting between them.

After packing up all the wedding presents and other paraphernalia, we headed back west for the long drive to Vancouver. We did not stop overnight but went straight through — a fifteen-hour drive. Once we arrived back at our Broadway apartment and unloaded the car, I walked down to the Kentucky Fried Chicken restaurant that was close by and purchased a bucket of chicken and fries, and we consumed the handy dinner. I lived to regret it. I came down with an extreme case of food poisoning that night and was laid up for days, painting the walls with projectile vomit. A fine start to married life. I did not eat KFC for many years after that.

# CHAPTER 17

# Pharaoh's

Shortly after the wedding, desperate for a summer job to prepare for my second year at school, I had a major breakthrough that set me on a whole new path. I was given a DJ residency at Pharaoh's nightclub at the entrance to Gastown — an old part of Vancouver that had been restored to a tourist area. The club was one of the longest running in the city and well respected. Once again I was lucky enough to fall under the guidance of smart and professional club owners: Roger Gibson and Harvey Izen. (In the eighties they opened Richard's on Richards, which became one of Vancouver's top night spots.) Pharaoh's, which was down a flight of stairs, below ground, was a successful live venue that had converted to disco. Gone were the stage and shag carpets, replaced by steel and chrome, a mirror ball, art deco decor, and a specially designed DJ booth at the top of the small, but highly polished, dance floor. It was a club with a regular clientele. The bosses also owned a distinctive automobile that was often seen racing across town, promoting the Pharaoh's name. It was a stylish red-and-white modern motor in the design of an old gangster car, something Bonnie and Clyde might have driven, with the club's name emblazoned across the back. Harvey or the club manager, whose nickname was "Wedgie," would often be seen driving the impressive car. It was a sexy and seductive advertisement for the club.

To oversee the transition to an all-disco format, Roger and Harvey had discovered a Quebec DJ in Los Angeles. His name was Yvon Lefebvre. Yvon worked the star party circuit in Hollywood. He was in his thirties, and his style was very much old skool. But what he could do brilliantly was read a room. He knew what music the crowd wanted. He was so good at what he did that Roger and Harvey brought him up to Vancouver to launch the new and reimagined Pharaoh's. It was Yvon who hired me and aided in my DJ education.

It was the summer of 1976, and the world was focused on Canada and the Montreal Olympics. There was a party atmosphere across the whole country. Despite the disco backlash from music purists (bumper stickers with slogans such as "Support Your Local Musicians" and "Disco Sucks" were popular), the scene became incredibly successful. Hornby Street became the centre of Vancouver nightlife, with such clubs as Sugar Daddy's, Misty's, and the Candy Store all doing roaring business. On Georgia Street, the Loose Caboose in the Ritz Hotel was a hot spot. Annabelle's in the Four Seasons Hotel attracted an uptown suit crowd, as did the Air Affair on Pender Street, with fake hot air balloons hanging from the ceiling and the DJ booth in the cockpit of a mock plane. Clubs such as the Gandydancer and the Luv-a-Fair (later to become the top new wave club in the city) catered to Vancouver's large gay scene and also earned reputations as the most musically progressive discos in the city. Technically minded DJs such as Larry Bauder, Robyn Durling, and Richard Evans came to be known to not just other DJs, such as myself, but also the audience, who came to appreciate their expertise. At first there was a huge chasm between the straight clubs and the gay scene, as this was still a time when the sexual orientation lines were not blurred, and you never went to a gay club unless you were of that persuasion. But as disco progressed in popularity, those lines became blurred. Disco helped speed up the sexual revolution, for if you were in search of the best party you invariably ended up at a club that was sexually ambiguous. But in 1976 that was still a few years away from happening.

As for me, Pharaoh's became incredibly popular and there were lineups snaking their way up the basement stairs and spilling out onto the street, the area known as "the entrance to Gastown," Thursday through Saturday. On the nights when Yvon was the DJ, he would start off his set with the song "A Fifth of Beethoven" by Walter Murphy. It was a disco-ized version of the Fifth Symphony by the famous classical composer. The song was a number one hit. Yvon would stand in his booth, wearing his stylish suit, facing the audience, and pretend to conduct. It was pure showmanship, and the crowd loved it. It got the people dancing. The club's playlist at the time included such classic hits as "ABC" by the Jackson 5, as well as the disco hits of the moment, such as "Play That Funky Music" by Wild Cherry and Donna Summer's "Love to Love You Baby" — the LP version of that throbbing, orgasmic track (produced by Giorgio Moroder, who would help lay the foundation for electronic dance music or EDM) was over sixteen minutes long. It wasn't the first discotheque hit that featured heavy breathing and lascivious insinuation; there had been "Je t'aime … moi non plus" by Jane Birkin and Serge Gainsbourg in 1969, "Jungle Fever" by the Chakachas in 1971, and two years later, "Pillow Talk" by Sylvia Robinson (who would later establish Sugar Hill Records, the pioneering hip hop label). But Donna Summer's sexy opus, with its incredible production, became the first truly disco record that captured the pulse of what a modern nightclub was all about. The success of that song and album also helped establish Casablanca Records, run by Neil Bogart, as the premier disco label. The label's roster included not only Donna Summer, who would become disco's most successful artist, but also Kiss and the Village People. The label became famous not just because of its artists but also because of its outrageous promotional parties and lavish spending, and stories of a business fuelled by cocaine.

The idea of having a high-quality continuous soundtrack, with no interruption to its false reality, became the defining element of modern discotheques. That was made possible with the aid of the technically crisp audio of the twelve-inch single and its instrumental breaks. It would be Tom Moulton who invented the twelve-inch single, as it turns out, by accident. He was at the New York pressing plant Media Sound in order to get a test pressing of one of his productions. That particular day they had run out of seven-inch vinyl. To facilitate Moulton's requirements, the Media Sound engineer came to a compromise and pressed the single on twelve-inch vinyl, normally used only for albums. When Moulton saw the final pressing, with the grooves of the single bunched up together on the large piece of virgin vinyl, he asked if there was any way to spread out the grooves, which the engineer did. The result was a wider groove for the turntable stylus to sit in, producing a hot and higher pressing with increased volume, perfect for discotheques. Tom then added to the concept when he, and other producers, created instrumental breaks in the body of a song, extending it from three minutes to five or six minutes. This was a turning point in the disco revolution.

The first twelve-inch vinyl records were made commercially available that summer of 1976. One of the first was "Ten Percent" by Double Exposure on the Salsoul label, with a remix by Walter Gibbons. For the first time, a record was released and marketed specifically to the nightclub DJ and hard core fan. With only one song per side, extended by instrumental breaks, it allowed the stylus to sit snuggly and safely in the deep grooves, creating a richer, deeper bass sound. The thumping 4/4 beat was the key to motivating people to get up out of their seats and take to the dance floor. One confusing factor was the speed of the disc: some were 33 rpm, while others were 45 rpm. This would sometimes cause professional embarrassment for the DJ who forgot to change speed on the turntable to accommodate the incoming record. Eventually, the 45 rpm record became the norm. At Pharaoh's, the large bass bin speakers lined the side of the dance floor. Their tops were converted to a side bar, where patrons could sit and enjoy their drinks. But a small ridge had to be added, as the vibrations of the amplified sound from the giant speakers beneath caused the cocktail glasses and beer bottles to "walk" off the edge and crash onto the floor. The extended instrumental break in a song, at either the beginning, the middle, or the end, allowed the DJ to match the beats perfectly with the incoming song and seamlessly mix one cut into another. Turntables, such as the Technics 1200, allowed for a change in pitch control, and so the DJ could speed up or slow down a song to match the tempo. This was the birth of the technically minded DJ, eliminating the old style of talk-over, allowing the music to run uninterrupted from doors open to doors closed.

It was at this point that any disco DJ worth their salt learnt how to mix properly: counting beats per minute (BPM) using a stopwatch and listing that song and its BPM number in the playlist notebook. By referring to the notes, a DJ could seamlessly segue from one song into another. Once that skill had been mastered, then some audio tricks could be applied. For example, by playing a second copy of the same song on the other turntable, in sync with its twin, and setting the output so that both records were heard and then slightly increasing and decreasing the pitch, a phasing effect occurred. Or, what came to be known as "double beating" — once again, by using a second copy of the same song but lagging it a beat or two behind the main copy, an echo effect could be created just for key moments in the tune, such as "Dance, dance, dance…. Dance, dance, dance." All clever stuff with turntables and vinyl. Record companies even began to note the BPM on the labels of dance-oriented tracks, aiding the DJ's selection.

There was also a certain psychology and manipulation of the crowd used to increase revenue. Sometimes if the lineups were extremely long, management would ask me to play slow songs in an effort to turn over the crowd. Slow dancing was the antithesis of high-energy disco, but for those guys who wanted an excuse to ask a girl to dance, ballads did the trick. If a hundred people left, a hundred new patrons, each paying the cover charge, could be allowed to enter. Those new patrons would also immediately buy a drink. For those people who remained and who had met someone new, the first question after dancing together was, "Can I buy you a drink?" — once again, increasing revenue. "We are in the business of selling good times, booze, and sex," Roger explained to us once at a staff meeting, adding, "but not necessarily in that order."

Mick came to visit from England and stayed with us. It was great to see him, but, true to form, Air Canada lost his suitcase with all his stylish clothes as well as some personal items. It was never recovered. The airline was willing to reimburse him for only a fraction of the cost of his luggage and contents, just enough to buy underwear, socks, and so on. It put the boot in on his holiday experience. And, of course, Vancouver was nothing like Benidorm. But he did love hanging out at Pharaoh's and was chuffed to see me doing well at the gig. He returned to England, and I never saw him again.

Things were going well for Lily and me. I was thrilled with my role as a DJ and was earning okay money. I was just about to go into my second year of university. Lily had landed a clerical job as an accounts clerk. We were married. We were having fun. Life was good, and we were confident. So much so that Lily and I decided we needed another adventure. We should go to Australia.

# CHAPTER 18

# Australia

In addition to my DJ duties at night, I had taken on a second job in the daytime — selling tickets to tourists for sightseeing tours around Vancouver on old London double-decker buses. I guess my English accent helped me secure the gig. It was an honest and simple company run by two UBC business grad students. One of them even did double duty and drove the bus when one of their regular drivers was sick. They were good guys, full of youthful energy and commitment, and aggressive in tackling their long-established and respected business competitor, Gray Line Tours. They had bought a half-dozen 1950s British buses, done their best to refurbish them, and upgraded the tired engines. Their plan was to capitalize on the Vancouver summer tourist market, which was growing year by year as the world discovered the beautiful city on the "left coast." However, the buses would invariably break down, and things would be as unpredictable as the West Coast weather.

The office was an old, red stationary bus whose engine could not be revived, so it found another lease on life parked beside the luxurious and famous Bayshore Inn. I was stationed inside the bus beside a makeshift desk, answering the phone, selling tickets to the customers who wandered over from the hotel, and trying to appease tourists who were stranded in Stanley Park when inevitably one of the double-deckers gave up its old English ghost. Working with tourists can sometimes be as frustrating as it is comical, as if travellers leave common sense at home along with their gas bills. One time I had an American couple pay me for a pair of tickets, and I gave them their change in Canadian dollar bills. "Haven't you got any real money?" they asked me, with all seriousness. Another time, while riding on one of the tours with the customers, a man jumped up out of his seat to stop the bus as if it was actual city transit. He pulled what he thought was the cord to ring the request bell. However, the cord was in fact the electrical wire that connected the loudspeaker system so that the driver could provide his sightseeing commentary. He ripped it out of one of the speakers, muting the entire PA. The rest of the journey was completed in silence. I can't remember whether we had to refund the customers their money. On occasional hot days, some tourists inevitably asked me if the old buses had air conditioning. My young bosses had given me a pat answer by way of response: No, the buses don't have air conditioning, but they do have flow-through ventilation. (Read: the front and back windows were open.)

Occasionally I was on the Burrard Street sidewalk in a makeshift booth, or sometimes standing on the corner outside the Hotel Vancouver. It was illegal to solicit business, but you could sell tour tickets if a customer approached you. My quick-thinking young bosses manufactured a yellow oversized badge that said "Ask Me" to pin to my jacket. I had more than a few people ask me for all kinds of things. Sometimes they would even ask me for sightseeing tour tickets! It was not the most glamorous of jobs, but the wage, combined with what I was earning at Pharaoh's, plus Lily's paycheque at her clerical office job, proved more than seductive. By September we had accumulated more money than we had ever possessed in our lives. This got us thinking. Lily was anxious to see her homeland, and I was keen for another adventure. How about we move to Australia? So we made plans to go down under. Not just an obvious destination such as Melbourne or Sydney, but Perth, on the other side of the continent.

I cancelled my enrolment at UBC and applied for a second year transfer to the University of Western Australia in Perth (as a backup, I also applied to the universities in Sydney and Melbourne). I worked both jobs all the way through to Thanksgiving in October. When the tourist season was over, I concentrated on my DJ gig at Pharaoh's until the end of November.

What few items we owned we sold, except, of course, my ever-growing record collection. I shipped that to Australia weeks before we left. In order to prevent damage to the vinyl, I built a wooden crate three feet by three feet, and eighteen inches deep. I nailed steel edging on all four sides, and secured metal handles on its sides to allow for lifting. Once filled with LPs and singles, it was incredibly heavy. But it was solid. It had to be. The crate was going to go west across the Pacific via ship to Lily's aunt in Melbourne, not Perth, because we had no address of our own. The journey for the crate would take about three months. As for us, we flew in the opposite direction via London, England. Not only did this give me a chance to see my parents, but it was also cheaper than flying the obvious route directly across the Pacific. That was because the Canadian dollar was strong at the time, worth almost 10 percent more than the U.S. dollar, so we bought relatively cheap tickets to the U.K. and then planned to buy our tickets to Perth when we were in London.

We arrived in London in early December 1976. One of the topics dominating conversation was a sensational TV interview that had occurred on the first day of that month. A headline in the *Daily Mirror* captured the moment and the memory: "The Filth and the Fury!" It was a live interview by Thames TV host Bill Grundy with a young band talking about a new style of music and attitude. It was the notorious Sex Pistols and the famous TV interview, with its profanity, feigned boredom, and deliberate refusal to "play the game," that launched a musical revolution: punk rock.

Friends and family asked me about this new "punk rock" thing. I had never heard of it, and paid it no heed. It was the antithesis of the music that I was immersed in. Disco was beginning to dominate the pop culture world with not only its sound but also its fashion, its lifestyle, and its hedonistic attitude. Disco maestro Barry White summed it up perfectly when he said that the consumer was the star. That was what was in ascendency at the time — not this new thing called punk, with its anti-establishment, anti-consumer attitude. Or so I thought.

After spending Christmas and New Year's with my family, Lily and I once again set off on our travels. We boarded a plane at Heathrow bound for Perth, Australia. In a strange coincidence, we landed at Bahrain to refuel. We were allowed to deplane and waited in the airport terminal away from the searing heat. It's the only time I have ever revisited my birthplace, but of course the only thing I could experience was the heat, the high-priced snacks in the cool waiting area, and the Arabic residents dressed in their traditional clothes. The next leg of the journey took us to a stopover in Asia (Thailand, I believe), where we picked up lots of Australian tourists, predominately men on a break from their factory jobs. I knew that piece of info because they would shout out the names of their bosses and the companies they worked for, telling the whole plane their thoughts on their vocations and their corporate leaders, as they ordered more in-flight beers. And it wasn't flattering. They proceeded to drink one "tinny" after another until we landed in Perth. Welcome to Oz!

Perth is a beautiful city. It actually lies slightly inland on the Swan River, which links it to the port of Fremantle. At that time the world had not yet discovered this jewel on the Indian Ocean. It is also incredibly isolated, over a thousand miles away from its nearest major neighbour, Adelaide in South Australia. Perth's population at the time was only about five hundred thousand people. You could lose yourself there, no problem. Yachts on the river and ships on the sea were as common as cars and trucks on the road. Lily and I found an apartment close to Cottesloe Beach in an area called Mosman Park, just north of Fremantle and west of Perth. It was idyllic. The campus of Western Australia was about 45 minutes away by bus, but it was manageable. And what a beautiful campus it was, with luscious walkways covered in flowers and all kinds of vegetation. The blue waters of the Swan River gleamed close by. One of the first things I did was check in with the registration officials on campus. But there was a hitch. They could not confirm my transfer. There was some kind of holdup with the paperwork.

I was not too concerned, as I was confident that things would work out before classes started in late February. We filled our days by exploring Perth and spending time at the nearby sandy beaches. The beach was central to the lifestyle of the area, so much so that just as you entered the apartment there was a low foot shower to wash off the sand from your feet. How civilized. And then something extraordinary happened. To fill the empty hours, I began to write poetry. I had absolutely no idea where this sudden urge to be creative came from. I was not academically inclined, or so I believed, and I certainly was not bookish. Other than the poems I had to read as a schoolboy or in my English 100 course at UBC, poetry was alien to my world. But for some reason it began to flow out of me. It was as if an unknown relative had turned up at the apartment one day, unannounced, and had taken up residency in the corner of the room. The empty space was filled with unusual chatter. I listened. I wrote. Not amazing stuff, but it was stuff, and I continued to let it flow, not knowing the source. It kept me busy while I waited for the pieces of life's jigsaw to fall into place.

I then received some bad news. The University of Western Australia could not confirm that I would be able to start classes come the start of the new school year. Our plans were not fitting together, and we began to second-guess ourselves. Lily was anxious to see her hometown of Melbourne and reconnect with her family and friends. I was determined to lock in something significant. So we made a decision to move once again. After just one month in Perth, we journeyed on to Melbourne in anticipation of my registering at the University of Victoria.

We stayed at Lily's aunt and uncle's house for a couple of days, and then once again lucked out by securing an apartment in the trendy area of South Yarra. I connected with the registration office at the university. Once again, there was confusion with the paperwork and I was asked to be patient. Meanwhile, the University of Western Australia had contacted me and said that I was all clear to register for the second year there. Even Sydney University accepted me. But it was too late. We were here now, and money was running out. Then I received the bad news that the University of Victoria was not going to offer me a place. I was pissed off.

I set about finding work and scanned the want ads in *The Age*. One of them was an invitation to a creative seminar, with a guarantee of a job in the literary world. Thinking my new poetic urge might lead me to a job and a paycheque, I turned up to a meeting in a hotel boardroom. I sat in the back of the room, which was filled with about twenty other prospective job seekers waiting on folding chairs for the team leader to arrive. When he did eventually take his place standing in front of our unemployed souls, he made a heartfelt speech that would have made Dale Carnegie proud. The pitch was for door-to-door encyclopedia salespeople. Sell a batch, and you get a commission. I felt like standing on the street corner with an "Ask Me" badge was better than this situation. I immediately jumped up, voiced my disapproval for the sham, and walked out of the "class." I was quickly followed by almost all the other unemployed folks. The manager gave me a death stare, and I could see I had been branded a troublemaker. After a series of more legitimate interviews, I was offered a clerical job in a respected and well-known company. The man who did the hiring asked me to call back later that day to get the details of my start date and other relevant info. Lily and I arranged to go out for a late afternoon meal to celebrate, using what meager funds we had. Once again, things did not go as planned. While we were waiting for our food orders to arrive, I excused myself and went to a public phone booth to call my future employer to obtain details of the position. He apologized profusely, and said that after deliberation with his bosses they felt that they could not give the job to "a new Australian." I had been unhired. I returned to the dinner table to give Lily the bad news. We ate the expensive meal anyway.

It did not help matters when one day, while crossing the road, a sharpie (Australia's version of a skinhead) who was walking in the opposite direction began to ogle Lily in an ugly way and uttered a few suggestive comments. Given the recent frustration in our lives, I lost my temper and turned around to confront the guy. We started to snarl at each other right there in the middle of the busy road. Luckily, Lily dragged me away. I would have gotten killed, if not by the fight then by the cars that were ready to take off when the lights turned green.

Once again, it seemed the universe was playing with us. This time, it was throwing barriers along this Australian path as if it was telling us to return to Vancouver and our Canadian destiny. So we said our goodbyes to Lily's aunt and uncle, who had been kind enough to help us out. The day before we returned whence we came, my crate of records arrived at their terraced house. It was a particularly poetic comment on how things had turned out. The records would have to stay there, untouched, until they, too, could return home.

## CHAPTER 19

# The Beats

April was far from a cruel month to be back in Vancouver. The trees and grass were lush, daffodils were in bloom, temperatures were moderate, and residents strolled or rode their bicycles around the Stanley Park seawall. It was as if all was right with the world. I came to a realization: Canada is a great place to leave, but an even better place to come back to.

After Lily and I found a new apartment, we set about putting our lives back together. This was my eighth change of address in three years! With a new base of operations, I was able to organize the return of my records from Australia. I reapplied to UBC to resume my second-year studies. The poetic bug that had bit me while I was down under had fired up my brain in a good way, so I decided to pursue English studies. As for work, luckily Pharaoh's asked me to return to my DJ duties, and I spent many afternoon hours at the club doing my music homework, listening to all the key hits I had missed. It wasn't long till I was back in the nightclub groove. By early summer, my crate of vinyl arrived from Melbourne. It had gone all the way there and back without being opened or damaged. The same could not be said for our meager bank accounts.

The disco influence was everywhere at this time. It even made the evening news when celebrities were seen dancing and cavorting with unbridled abandon. In New York the most famous discotheque in the world opened its doors in April 1977 — Studio 54. It came to represent everything about the disco lifestyle. Sex could be found easily, hedonism was the objective, and the elite could rub shoulders and grind hips with the young and beautiful. Patrons lined up outside beyond the velvet rope, hoping to be picked for entrance by Steve Rubell, one of the co-owners. He would choose interesting characters, knowing that the perfect mix for a party atmosphere ran not just along gender or sexual lines but also along class and age lines. The rich danced with the poor, the old with the young, the straight with the gay, and the famous with the unknown. Studio 54 became symbolic of the decadent times. Everyone, it seemed, wanted entrance to this world. Life was a non-stop party. And the "zip-less fuck" (a term coined by feminist writer Erica Jong in her 1973 novel *Fear of Flying*), booze and cocaine, helped keep it going.

The elitist element of Studio 54 is reflected in the story of the creation of one of the most famous songs of the disco period. Chic band members Nile Rodgers and Bernard Edwards had lined up outside the club waiting to gain entrance. The androgynous singer Grace Jones had invited them to party with her. Chic's first single, "Dance, Dance, Dance (Yowsah, Yowsah, Yowsah)," was a major hit at every club across North America, including Studio 54. But the two musicians were refused entry to the club. Incensed, they went to their recording studio and channelled their anger into a song that had the hook "Fuck off." Knowing that they would not get the track played with such profanity, they changed the chorus to "Freak out." The song was released under the title "Le Freak," and it became one of the most successful tunes of the disco period.

In the summer of 1977, the owners of Pharaoh's started to expand their operations and opened a club in Palm Springs — Zelda's. A DJ exchange was arranged. I would go down there for two weeks, and Zelda's DJ would come to Vancouver to spin records at Pharaoh's. It was my first out-of-town gig in my young career. I was still only twenty-two years of age. My boss, who remained in Vancouver, gave me the keys to his house and his 1963 Thunderbird convertible. I remember stepping off the plane after it had landed in the desert and being overwhelmed by the heat. It was like walking into a hairdryer. Like every DJ, I carried with me those hit records that pack the dance floor, but I also brought with me a new album by a brand new band — the Village People. The first night at the club, with the crowded dance floor tight with the beautiful, rich set, I played the LP for the first time. The opening track, "San Francisco," was an instant hit, and as the song ended it melded beautifully into the second track, "In Hollywood (Everybody Is a Star)." The audience stopped dancing, not to leave the floor but to applaud me — the DJ — for the mix. I hadn't done a thing but let the record play, but it was the first time that I became aware of how the audience appreciated DJ skills.

It was a wild time to be in Palm Springs, and Zelda's was the number one club. Sex, drugs, and money were seemingly woven into the leisure lives of the residents and the many tourists. The town was brimming with beautiful people and tales of mafia connections, wild parties, and outrageous behaviour — stories of DJs receiving blow jobs in the booth, and the rich and elderly claiming young men and women as their desert distractions. One day one of the guys, an overly handsome chap who worked at the club, mentioned "ludes." I had no idea what he was talking about, so he expanded on the word — Quaaludes.

"What are they?" I asked innocently.

"They're a downer," he replied.

"Why would anyone want to take a downer?" I asked, but he just smiled and walked away, arm in arm with his gorgeous girlfriend, who was a waitress at the club. They were both aspiring models waiting to be discovered, and partied long into the desert night after their shifts were finished at Zelda's. Palm Springs was an exotic way station for the young and beautiful who were waiting for the train of success to arrive. And those of senior years who had alighted from that ride, at this, their final stop, were willing to share their advantages with those they bestowed their favours upon.

My two weeks were short enough not to get into too much trouble, and my time behind the turntables was a success. So much so that management asked me if I would consider staying in Palm Springs full-time. However, having screwed up my education with the Australia trip, I needed to get back to Vancouver to enrol in university, and I realized that if I stayed in that party town I might not get out alive. And so I returned to Pharaoh's, university, and my books and records.

Roger, my boss at the club, had an elderly aunt who was anxious to sell her car. It was an old green Acadian that she hardly used. I could have it for five hundred dollars, he told me. And so I bought it, and named the jalopy Archie. He was not the most beautiful of cars, but he was reliable, even if he did have a musty smell from a leaky back window. Archie had what car buffs called "three in the tree" — the gear stick was mounted on the steering column and had only three speeds: go, reverse, and neutral. That's all I needed. I no longer had to catch the last bus home after my DJ set. That was a relief. It also gave Lily and me a chance to explore British Columbia. One of the great discoveries we made was Vancouver Island. The stories from friends, and the tourist pamphlets plucked from information booths, all remarked on how gorgeous it was, but, as it turns out, that was an understatement. We drove down to Tsawwassen, drove Archie onto the ferry, and sailed over to Victoria. It was, like so many things in Canada during that period, a step back in time. The city brought to mind the famous years of the Empire, and there was a feeling that Victoria was more British than Britain itself. We spent the night in the famous Empress Hotel. The hotel still served tea and crumpets in the late afternoon. I found that amusing.

The following day we headed out on Highway 4 to the west coast of the island. The route took us through the luscious Cathedral Grove of giant cedar trees, many of them over eight hundred years old. It was a spiritual experience, journeying through the green, wet canopy held high by spectacular limbs of timber that pointed skywards like earthly messengers toward heaven. The place lived up to its name — it induced reverence. No wonder the distinctive Haida art, which I had become attracted to, embodied the natural spirit. That spirit was infused everywhere within this landscape. The road continued west toward Long Beach and the Pacific Rim National Park. We had heard stories of how, in the hippie days, this was a destination for the psychedelic initiates, and how it was a place you could quite agreeably get lost in. As it turns out, there was a historical truth to this. In days past some vessels had been shipwrecked on that coast, and the marooned sailors had washed up on the beach. To find their way back to civilization, they had had to make their way through the dense rainforest, some never to be seen again.

After securing a campsite (we did not have a tent, but planned to sleep in Archie), we looked on with delight at the spectacular beach and its ferocious waves whipped high by strong Pacific winds, crashing with thunder on the rocks. The beach itself, with its flat, golden sand, stretched for sixteen kilometres. It was easily the most wonderful sight I had ever seen. There was hardly anyone else around. Twilight was approaching, so we gathered driftwood to start a fire and cook the few food items that we had brought with us. We selected an area out of the wind, behind a small cove. With the flames entertaining us and the food feeling fine in our empty bellies after the four-hour journey, we relaxed into this most incredible place. After a short while, I ventured out from behind the dark cove and wandered barefoot down to the water. As I turned the corner, into the remaining light of the twilight sky, I was overwhelmed. The eastern horizon was smeared with a multitude of brilliant colours: yellow, gold, red, orange, and blue. Quickly, I called to Lily to witness this majestic display before the evening sun disappeared like a passing prophet into the vast Pacific. We watched in wonder until darkness filled the infinite sky. If we had stayed in the shadows by the warmth of the fire, we would have been oblivious to this gift of creation. There was a lesson to be learned there. The following day we returned to Vancouver, but the joy of Long Beach was etched in our hearts like initials of love carved into the trunk of a cedar tree. In my mind, Long Beach and Pacific Rim National Park is one the great wonders of the world. We were lucky enough to visit it before it was discovered by the twenty-first-century Expedia crowd. We journeyed back there as often as we could.

That September I started my second year at UBC. It turned out to be pivotal, especially because of one English professor: Warren Tallman. I was shocked when he first entered the class that September. He was fragile — maybe a hundred and thirty-five pounds — and he chain smoked, lighting a new cigarette with what remained of the old one; he must have smoked a dozen or so during the course of his lectures, crushed butts appearing around the legs of his chair like squashed bugs. He had the shakes, possibly due to his love of Black Label beer, and an occasional smile brought to life by an inner secret like ashes fanned by a gentle breeze. Question: This was a man who was responsible for guiding young souls to healthy and productive lives? Answer: As it turns out, he also had a brilliant mind and an incredible poetic sense, and despite his apparent burnt-out nature, was still a creative force to be reckoned with. Professor Tallman was the embodiment of the subject he taught — the Beats. He was connected to many of the legendary founders of that revolutionary poetic group, and had been one of the individuals who had founded the UBC creative writing program. He had championed a Vancouver poetry movement called "Tish" (an anagram for "Shit"), had inspired such young new poets as bill bissett, and was the elder statesman of the West Coast modern poetry movement. This man knew his stuff.

One of the first assignments of Professor Tallman's class was to read the book *On the Road* by Jack Kerouac. Having turned my back on reading during my teen years, I had never heard of the literary work, let alone read it. It had a profound effect on me and, as it turns out, a whole generation of readers. Through that book I discovered Neal Cassady, who was not only the manic inspiration for the character of Dean Moriarty but also, in real life, drove Ken Kesey and the Merry Pranksters' bus, "Further," as it careened across America in 1964. My world of pop culture was intersecting with my studies. I was fascinated. Years later, when I was hosting the rock 'n' roll news for MuchMusic, I interviewed Carolyn Cassady, Neal's widow and Jack's friend, when she visited Toronto to publicize her book *Off the Road*. I made the unusual gesture of buying her flowers and presenting them to her before we sat down to chat. She was flattered. It was the least I could do for a woman who had inspired two important members of the Beat Generation, and had indirectly inspired me.

One of the other books that would change me was Colin Wilson's *The Outsider*. When this book was first published in 1956, it caused a sensation. Wilson's premise, using both fictional and real-life characters as examples, was that certain individuals "see too much, too deeply, and too far," and as such become outsiders to mainstream society. They are forever on a quest to add meaning to a life that flips between long periods of emptiness and short, intense moments of joy and insight. Wilson was hailed as a literary genius when the book was published, and he was bracketed in with the Angry Young Men movement of the British literary world. The fact that he was sleeping rough in Hyde Park at night and studying at the British Museum reading room during the day only added to Wilson's myth. There was a rock 'n' roll aspect to this new creative hero. As he commented, "How extraordinary my fame should coincide with Elvis Presley's." His star would later fall as fast as it had risen, but for me, and many others, his outsider theory remained important.

I was also introduced to Malcolm Lowry's book *Under the Volcano* — one man's descent into alcoholic oblivion during Mexico's Day of the Dead. The work, and the story behind it, was fascinating in itself, but then I discovered that Lowry, an expat Englishman, had lived in a shack in Dollarton, on the way to Deep Cove in North Vancouver. So a road trip was organized, and Lily and I made the pilgrimage to where he once had lived. During his time there, a fire had destroyed the home and some of his manuscripts. He had returned to England, where he died an alcoholic, but *Under the Volcano* is considered one of the great works of the twentieth century. It all seemed very rock 'n' roll to me.

Through my class essays and poetry assignments, Professor Tallman became interested in my unusual life. He was fascinated by my time with the Inuit, my travels across Canada, and my DJ life, and he was especially fascinated by the fact that Lily and I had come from opposite corners of the world and had somehow crossed paths. He organized gatherings at his house with his wife, Ellen; other writers and students were invited, and Lily and I were honoured to be invited as well. We were the outsiders — non-academic, young, and creatively naive — but somehow we fit in and enjoyed the events we attended. It was there that we met the acclaimed poet Allen Ginsberg, Lawrence Ferlinghetti (the founder of San Francisco's City Lights Bookstore, which published the Beats), and other writers. I remember Professor Tallman explaining to his living room full of guests that despite his association with the Beats, drugs had no attraction for him. Beer was his joy. But he said that he took LSD once in that very room. During the trip he placed his hands on the old, rough, burly timber beams that held up the ceiling and realized how patient they were — just waiting there, happy to be of use.

I was just a second-year student whose skills were limited, but Professor Tallman encouraged me to follow a creative path: "Just keep going, and you'll find it — whatever 'it' is that you are looking for."

It would be on Professor Tallman's recommendation that I eventually enrolled in the UBC creative writing program while I continued my English studies. I fell under the guidance of George McWhirter, a brilliant poet, as well as teacher. His first collection of poems was a winner of the Commonwealth Poetry Prize, and many years later he was named Vancouver's first poet laureate. He helped shape my poems and short stories. Poetry fascinated me, and I delved deeper into the subject. T.S. Eliot's poems such as *The Waste Land* and "The Love Song of J. Alfred Prufrock" were works of genius. (I learned "Prufrock" by heart.) The Romantic poets were hippies before their time. I became fascinated by the works and imagery of William Blake. I discovered that he had written the words to one of England's most famous hymns and one of my favourites: "Jerusalem." (We always sang that hymn at the end of every school term back in my Latymer days.) Blake was a visionary, literally and figuratively. It's no wonder his lines about "a world in a grain of sand" resonated with the psychedelic drug set.

There was hope for poetry in this modern age. By the end of the decade, poet-musicians such as John Cooper Clarke and Linton Kwesi Johnson added modern relevance to the ancient medium. One particular punk poet, based in New York, had gained media attention that cut across literary and musical boundaries — Jim Carroll. "Images sharp as broken glass," wrote one critic. I was impressed. I'd like to do that, I thought. But as I look back now, I realize that it's not what I wanted to be but what I *was* that counted. I *was* a DJ. It was as natural as my walks along English Bay. My youthful and half-formed aspirations for being a writer didn't even make it to the proverbial back seat of my imagination. They were eventually locked away in the trunk.

# CHAPTER 20

# Vancouver Summers

It's true that it rains a lot in Vancouver; in fact, there's an old West Coast saying that if you can see the mountains, it's just about to rain, and if you can't see them, then it is raining. But there is arguably no greater place to be in the world than in Vancouver when the weather co-operates and it's a hot summer. It's possible to swim in the morning, climb Grouse Mountain in the afternoon (and ski, if snow is still around), indulge in a fine meal in the evening, and then walk along English Bay at sunset.

Soccer had become incredibly popular in the city with the success of the Vancouver Whitecaps in the North American Soccer League. The team attracted thousands of fans to Empire Stadium with the likes of international players like the legendary English forward Alan Ball Jr., the South African goalkeeper Bruce Grobbelaar (later to go on to become a star at Liverpool), and Scottish wizard Willie Johnston (who once took a swig of beer from a fan while preparing to take a corner, much to the delight of the fans). When the high-flying and expensive New York Cosmos team visited, the stadium would be packed with thirty thousand people. In 1979 the Whitecaps played the Cosmos in the semi-finals of the playoffs and beat them in an incredibly exciting match. The city was transfixed. The game was televised on ABC television to the whole of North America, and respected commentator Jim McKay made the comment that "Vancouver must be like the deserted village right now." That did not go over well with those of us on the West Coast, and may have even sparked the team to greater efforts. The Whitecaps went on to win the Soccer Bowl. Tens of thousands of fans lined Robson Street for the victory parade. One banner read "The Village of Vancouver Salutes the #1 Champs." It had been a long time since the city could celebrate a championship-winning team.

To be employed in Vancouver nightlife (clubs, restaurants, bars) during the summer months afforded one the opportunity to indulge in the area's natural beauty during the weekdays when there were fewer people around. The crew from Pharaoh's, and many of the other clubs, congregated at Kitsilano Beach. It sometimes was like a nightclub in the sunshine and the sand. It was very much a jock beach, as there was a workout area close by, producing a constant parade of toned and bronzed bodies, both male and female, strutting around in their swim-wear. (The idea of working out at a gym was beginning to become fashionable.) Boom boxes played dance tunes, the rattle of dice in cups from numerous backgammon games could be heard, beverages were passed around, the smell of tobacco, marijuana, and suntan lotion was in the air, pickup games of soccer were organized on the grass behind the beach, tennis could be played if you could secure one of the free courts, and ice cream and other snacks were dispensed from the busy snack bar. If you were bored with sitting in the sun, not only could you swim in the Pacific Ocean, but you could also make the short walk to the magnificent Kitsilano open-air swimming pool that was close by. It was free, and it was of an enormous length. To sit on its deck and look across Burrard Inlet at The Lions mountain peaks, or out to the Pacific and the many ships at sea, was a more than satisfying visual, particularly after an energetic workout.

If you wanted to get adventurous with your tanning experience there was always Wreck Beach, the famous nudist area on the UBC campus. There was a steep unsupervised dirt path leading from the roadside through the woods and down to the water. Its entrance was slightly hidden, so you had to know where it was. This kept out many casual tourists. Visitors were greeted with a homemade sign nailed to a tree that stated that you had to carry out everything you had carried in, meaning you had to take your garbage with you. The beach, which had an air of being deserted, as the city left it to its own devices, was unregulated, and there were few visits from police or wardens. As such, there was an assertive group of local individuals who made sure that people honoured the place and took care of their litter, and that there weren't any stalkers or sex fiends lurking around. One of the other intriguing things was the entrepreneurial individuals who walked the beach nude, hawking their wares: "Marijuana, hashish, LSD ..." Customers had the option to bake on the inside as well as the outside while at Wreck Beach. The salesman's merchandise would be hidden in a fanny pack or a small cooler, unlike his personal tackle, which would dangle for all to see as he'd kneel down beside customers to complete the transaction.

Sometimes, when the weather was good, extended getaways were planned. One such trip concerned friends of ours who had rented a large cabin on one of the many gulf islands that lie between the mainland and Vancouver Island. Six of us were invited for a long weekend of fishing, water-skiing, barbecues, and beer. Lily and I packed our gear into Archie, drove to the docks, and caught the ferry across the strait. With a hand-drawn map in hand, we made our way to the spacious and well-equipped cabin and met up with our friends. It was a memorable time: Lily and I caught huge salmon, I learned to water-ski, although it took many attempts (I never realized how exhausting that sport is), and we spent the evenings eating, drinking, singing, and just having a wonderful West Coast time. But that was not the most memorable part of the short holiday. That Monday Lily and I set off before the others to make sure we returned to the mainland in time for me to DJ that night. There's limited space for cars on the ferry, and I did not want to miss the early sailing. We returned to the city with no problems, unlike our hosts, as we found out a day or two later.

After we left, our friends had dutifully cleaned the cabin, returning everything to its rightful place — the boat, the skis, the fishing tackle, the furniture, the dishes, and so on. As for garbage, visitors to the island were reminded to take their garbage with them, as there was garbage pickup only for those few residents who lived on the island permanently. Our friends had gathered their mixed refuse into one big twist-tied plastic bag; there was no room in the trunk, so those in the back seat made room for the smelly new cargo. They then set off to join the lineup of cars for the ferry back to Vancouver. On the way through the back roads, they spotted a garbage bin. Thinking it was a community depository, they figured it would be fine to just pull over and dump the offending bag. They did exactly that, and then carried on with their journey. By the time they arrived at the dock, many cars were lined up, with engines off, patiently waiting for the ferry to arrive. Our friends took their place in the queue, and waited. About forty-five minutes later they heard shouting close by. Then the offending garbage bag was loudly dumped beside their vehicle by an angry stranger. Those in cars close by stared at the commotion. As it turns out, the bin that they had used to deposit their garbage belonged to a private resident. The people had been so irate when they had seen their receptacle being used by some visiting city dweller (this had obviously happened to them before) that they had retrieved the bag, pulled it open, and sifted through its contents until they could find some telltale sign identifying the guilty party. As bad luck would have it, one of our friends had written the licence plate number of their car on a piece of paper (not sure why). *Ah ha*, the strangers had thought, *Got you!* After scooping up the garbage and stuffing it back into its bag, the strangers had driven to the ferry dock until they had spotted the vehicle. Words were exchanged, apologies made, innocence pleaded, and our embarrassed friends had to return to the city with the overpowering evidence of a grand weekend squashed into the back seat of their car.

When I was out enjoying the ocean and the walks I was able to secure occasional summer student work to supplement my DJ income. One particular gig stands out — the Vancouver Folk Festival. I was hired as a roadie and roustabout for the festival that took place at Jericho Beach, close to Kitsilano. The setting was spectacular, with the ocean and the mountains on the north side of the site. There was a buzz of excitement for all involved: the team was a collection of old West Coast hippies, passionate administrators, musicians, students, and a multitude of volunteers. Tents had to be erected, stages built, and wire picket fencing rolled out and put in place around the grounds. Putting up the tents was one of the most satisfying elements of the job, because it made you feel as if you were working in a circus, with all the romantic mythology attached. The festival had two distinct varieties of tents. There were regular oversized ones for performers and catering and dressing areas. But there was also a type of tent that was like a curved canopy, with distinctive red and white stripes on its waterproof covering. The frame of sturdy steel girders was bolted together, then the covering laced on. When all was ready, a group of about twenty people manned various ropes, the circular girding of the canopy was hauled about twenty metres into the air, and the apparatus would spread out its surface like a large eyelid. It had the potential for great danger if it fell apart or fell over, so we erected it carefully under the guidance of an experienced individual who shouted out orders about whether to pull or loosen the ropes. Once in place, the tent acted as the entrance to the festival. It was also the greatest advertisement for the event for those passing by, similar to today when you see the Cirque du Soleil big top.

Even though folk music was not my music of choice, the feeling of camaraderie and, of course, the performances couldn't help but make the working atmosphere one of delight. This was particularly so when the musicians held impromptu singalongs backstage for all those around. After the three-day festival was over, the team, and the tents, segued into another world-class event: the Vancouver Children's Festival. Not only did the gigs keep me busy and employed, but they also helped lay the groundwork for my knowledge of putting on a show that I utilized later on in the 1980s.

After the summer festival season was over, a big house party was staged in the suburbs. All the crew was there, including two individuals, a guy and a girl, who had worked alongside me for many days. They were slightly younger than me, nineteen or so, and I believe they were street kids who had been hired by the administrators to give disadvantaged youth the opportunity of employment. Unfortunately, the young man had fallen in love (or lust) with his female associate. The relationship had been broken off by the girl, but the young man was having none of it. He turned up to the party either on powerful drugs or having some form of mental breakdown. He turned violent toward anything and anyone in front of him. The bosses tried their best to calm him down and control the situation, but he appeared to be getting worse and more violent. In the end, emergency services were called. The young man's behaviour was so extreme that the ambulance attendants put him in a straitjacket and led him away. That was a sad and unsettling end to a glorious late summer.

# CHAPTER 21

# Saturday Night Fever

Music critics slagged disco for its repetitive sound, its shallow lyrics, and its inability to develop any real stars. There weren't any full-length albums that stood repeated listening. There were exceptions — most notably Donna Summer, Gloria Gaynor, KC and the Sunshine Band, and Barry White — but on the whole it was a singles market, literally, for the patrons as well as the artists who rode on the successes of one-off songs. There were hits such as "Play That Funky Music" by Wild Cherry, "Fly Robin Fly" by Silver Convention, or "Boogie Nights" by Heatwave, but the careers of those artists lasted for only a season and then fell like leaves in autumn. There was no longevity.

Just when it looked like disco might fade into the night, it received an incredible injection of vitality from the movie *Saturday Night Fever*, starring John Travolta. But it was not the first movie to cash in on the disco phenomenon. In 1975 the movie *Cooley High* was released. Although not a disco movie per se, it featured a stellar lineup of Motown music, as the film is set in Chicago 1964, and exploited the rise of emerging black culture. Despite a meager budget of less than a million dollars, and without any recognizable stars, it was a surprise hit. The movie grossed over thirteen million dollars at the box office. Its success lay in a lighthearted script that suddenly turns dark. Its simple story tapped into important elements of the times — gang violence, sexism, and the importance of education for inner city youth — all to the soundtrack of such artists as the Supremes, the Four Tops, and Stevie Wonder. It was, as they say, a sleeper hit.

The following year, in October 1976, the comedy *Car Wash* was released. This was more in tune with the disco times. It was not a success at the box office, but it did spawn one of the biggest hits of the decade, a song whose intro is still heard today at sporting events: "Car Wash" by Rose Royce. And then in December 1977 the whole world came down with a case of *Saturday Night Fever*. The movie and the soundtrack were a cultural phenomenon. The double album would go on to become one of the bestselling soundtracks of all time and spawn countless hits. There were such Bee Gees tunes as "Stayin' Alive" and "Night Fever," which became an anthem of sorts for nightclub life. Yvonne Elliman had the biggest hit of her career with the song "If I Can't Have You," as did the Trammps with the crowd-pleasing "Disco Inferno." The *Saturday Night Fever* soundtrack was, without a doubt, one of the greatest party records ever created. People who previously might not have ventured into a nightclub were now boosting numbers on weekend nights. TV shows as well as dance studios were giving disco dancing lessons. Disco, which six months earlier had appeared to be a future candidate for life support, was not only re-energized but also up and running on the musical equivalent of steroids.

One night in early 1978 a man called Paul Snider wandered into Pharaoh's. Dressed as a pimp, he billed himself as a club promoter and convinced the owners to stage a "John Travolta Dance-Alike" contest based on the movie *Saturday Night Fever*. Over the next couple of weeks, the staff worked with him on this promotion. I, in particular, had to work closely with him as he continually bugged me to interrupt the music to announce over the mic the forthcoming dance contest. The waitresses nicknamed him "Snake Eyes." Girls hung around him like users around a key of cocaine. Surprisingly the contest was a huge success, and he continued to be welcome at the club. He launched another club promotion, male strippers on ladies' night. I, of course, being the DJ playing the tunes for the show, had to be part of this burlesque. I remember one stripper giving me his list of three songs to program and telling me to give him five minutes' warning before showtime so that he could "warm up the machinery" in the washroom. Oh, the glamour of it all! (This idea of having male strippers at a dance club would eventually lead to Snider's creation of the Chippendales dancers.) Snider continued to stage a variety of promotional ideas, from magic shows to other dance contests, but they were all disappointing failures.

One night Snider came into the club and declared that he had discovered his future and she was serving in a Hastings Street Dairy Queen ice cream parlour. Her name was Dorothy Stratten. She was just eighteen years of age, and he was going to marry her and make her a star. Which he did. Their destiny took them to Los Angeles. Dorothy became the 1980 Playboy Playmate of the Year. But Ms. Stratten fell in love with movie director Peter Bogdanovich, and he with her. In a fit of jealous rage Snider blew her face off with a shotgun after he had tied her to a sex bondage chair, a prototype of his next entrepreneurial project, and had his way with her. He then turned the gun on himself. STAR 80 was Snider's vanity licence plate.

Five months after the success of *Saturday Night Fever*, Casablanca Records, which had now also branched out into the film business, hoped to continue the success of disco on the big screen by commissioning *Thank God Its Friday*. It was a flop. The movie appeared to be more of a vehicle to sell the soundtrack, but even the bloated triple album was not great, although it had some commercially successful tracks, most notably "Last Dance" by Donna Summer. That song became a must-play at discos all over the world (no surprise that it became the last song of the evening), and it also won an Oscar in 1978 for Best Original Song. In all honesty, that was the only good thing to come out of that movie.

The disco concept also married itself to another popular fad at the time — roller skating. The rinks were like discotheques with the dancers on wheels. There would be a mirror ball, a DJ, and suitable disco sportswear for the patrons. Two movies released in 1979 attempted to capture this new branch of the dance world: *Roller Boogie*, starring Linda Blair from *The Exorcist*, and *Skatetown, U.S.A.*, with Patrick Swayze, later to star in the 1980s mega-hit movie *Dirty Dancing*. Both soundtracks included "Boogie Wonderland" by Earth, Wind & Fire. But that was the only real hit on the *Roller Boogie* album. *Skatetown, U.S.A.* had the stronger disco selection, with such crowd favourites as the Jacksons' "Shake Your Body (Down to the Ground)," "Boogie Nights" by Heatwave, and the monster disco single "Born to Be Alive" by Patrick Hernandez. But both movies flopped badly. Disco, despite its ubiquitous influence, was becoming embarrassing, and it was on its last dance, if not its last legs.

# CHAPTER 22

# I Will Survive

Even though the revolutionary sound of punk and new wave was beginning to make a dent in the disco facade by the end of the decade, disco still had a huge influence — in music, fashion, and advertising. On Fridays after work, during cocktail hour, every lady who entered Pharaoh's was presented with a rose. There were wet T-shirt contests, special promotions with beer companies, and fashion shows — anything to keep the momentum going and to fill the space, especially early on weeknights. And if you could convince celebrities to visit the club, even better.

Members of the Vancouver Canucks hockey team regularly frequented Pharaoh's, and there are two vivid memories I have of the team. The first is when they played the New York Islanders and some of the Islander players accompanied the Canucks to the club. During an especially successful moment in the evening, when the crowd had packed the dance floor, I looked over and there was legendary netminder Chico Resch at the top of the small stairs that led to the fire escape with a huge smile on his face, obviously enjoying himself and the music. I was honoured. The other memory is not as cheerful. One night an individual whom I had never seen before in the club entered into an argument with one of the Canucks. He had a lot of friends, but he didn't realize that there was a whole hockey team to back up his opponent. Words were exchanged. And the next thing that happened was an all-out brawl featuring twenty or so people. Somebody raised a Heineken bottle to smash over the head of somebody else. I vividly remember seeing that green bottle being raised high above the melee and fully expecting blood to be splattered all over the dance floor. Luckily, one of the bartenders came running out from behind the bar and grabbed the man before a fatal blow could be delivered. As for me in the DJ booth, I looked on with powerless amazement and put on a love song (possibly "Reunited" by Peaches & Herb), thinking that might calm the fighters down, but then quickly realized the best thing was silence.

On one particular slow evening early in the week, I smelled smoke and spied flames coming from one of the enclosed seating areas close to my DJ booth. The club doorman and manager were in the office, occupied with something more stimulating than an early evening half-empty club, and so I rushed to where the flames were coming from. Inside the enclosed space was a gang of guys who, through boredom, had collected a pile of matchbooks (before the club opened, it was the waitresses' job to place a set of Pharaoh's matchbooks in every ashtray in the club) and set them alight. Being a basement club, the flames could have ignited the tiles, dust, and wiring on the low ceiling. Luckily they did not, and I managed to douse the flames and, in the process, call the gang something more than simple idiots. I returned to my booth and prepared to cue the next record. At that moment the leader of the gang stepped onto the empty dance floor, gave me the finger, and shouted abuse. Emotion overrode common sense, and I stormed out of my area and tackled the guy. While we were on the floor wrestling, the remainder of his crew was kicking me in the stomach. The fight lasted only a short time, but it seemed like forever before the doorman and manager arrived to rescue me and eject the gang. After dusting myself down and declaring that I had broken no bones, I resumed my music duties. After the club closed the doorman escorted me to my car in case the gang was waiting for me in the dark Gastown alleys. Mentally it shook me up, but I appeared to have escaped with little damage. However, later that week I was watching the NFL on TV when I sneezed. I ended up writhing on the apartment floor. The pain in my side was excruciating. I had broken my ribs. It turned out that the kicking I had taken had cracked my ribs significantly but not completely, and then the force of the sneeze had caused them to snap. It was one of the most painful things I have ever endured. After a visit to the hospital, where I turned the air royal blue with profanity as the nurses asked me to roll over for X-rays, and a couple of weeks of rest, I was okay to resume my gig and my classes.

The backlash toward disco took its toll on the lifestyle. Social behaviour revolved around the clubs. It defined your group of friends, your clothes, and to some degree, your sexual partners. An inordinate belief to keep partying every night, despite encroaching tough times, could not last.

Established rock bands and artists like the Rolling Stones, who released a dance twelve-inch remix of their song "Miss You" and Rod Stewart with "Da Ya Think I'm Sexy?" were using the disco style to colour their music, which seemed to be the death knell for true dance culture. Even Vancouver's Bryan Adams's first single, "Let Me Take You Dancing," released in 1979, was a disco track.

Two new styles of music began to infiltrate the dance scene and be added to a DJ's playlist. In late 1979 "Rapper's Delight" by the Sugarhill Gang became a huge club hit. It used a sample from Chic's "Good Times" to create a clever dance record. Not only was it the first commercially successful rap record, but it was also the first top forty hit to be available only as a twelve-inch 45 single. If that tune owed its creation to African-American New York neighbourhoods, the other new style of music to emerge owed its influence to predominately disillusioned white kids experimenting with art, technology, and the medium of pop. It was influenced by punk but was not aggressive in its attitude. It was, however, quirky and musically adventurous. It was new wave, and songs like "Hit Me with Your Rhythm Stick" by Ian Dury and the Blockheads, "Ça Plane Pour Moi" by Plastic Bertrand, and "Planet Claire" by the B-52s added a new dimension to the evening's proceedings. Disco played an important role in the development of new wave. The songs were played on only a few progressive North American radio stations, such as CFNY in Toronto. So the only place you could hear the tunes with any regularity (other than in your friend's basement) was at nightclubs. The Vancouver punk and new wave scenes had also captured media attention with such bands as D.O.A. and the Pointed Sticks. In addition to my regular disco hits that I had to search out, I was also buying new wave import records from the U.K. in such stores as Quintessence Records on West 4th Avenue and Ernie's Hot Wax on Davie Street. Needless to say, when the tunes were played they attracted a certain kind of dance fan, with their punky moves and dress.

One night in October 1979 a *Vancouver Sun* photographer came down to the club and took a photo of three of the new wave dancers. The next day there was a story in the paper about the death of disco and how "new wave punk rockers" were taking over Pharaoh's in Gastown. Roger, my boss, called a meeting. I tried to explain that the disco bubble was going to burst. New wave was going to be the pin that pricked that bubble. He agreed that there was a new musical movement happening but, of course, that new direction did not attract a well-dressed, moneyed crowd. He could not make a profit with that clientele. I understood. But the music had affected me. There was no going back. I could not un-hear what had been heard, or un-change what had been changed. Roger laid it out straight: either stop playing new wave music or lose my job. I lost my job. And disco had lost its cultural footing.

On July 12, 1979, there had been the Disco Demolition Night in Chicago at Comiskey Park stadium, when thousands of baseball fans were invited to witness a crate full of disco records being blown up. However, the promotion backfired when hundreds of fans stormed the field. The playing surface was ruined not only by the fans but also because of the fire. The Chicago White Sox had to forfeit the game. In early February 1980, the most well-known discotheque in the world, New York's Studio 54, was shut down. The owners, Steve Rubell and Ian Schrager, were jailed for tax evasion. Later that month at the 22nd Annual Grammy Awards in Los Angeles, Gloria Gaynor was given the award for Best Disco Recording for the song "I Will Survive." It was the first and last time such an award was handed out. In a wonderful piece of musical poetry, Gloria Gaynor's hits bookended the whole disco period. She had the first major disco recording, "Never Can Say Goodbye," and the last, "I Will Survive."

I had also survived my university studies. In April 1980 I graduated from the University of British Columbia with a degree in English. Disco had paid my way through school. My parents travelled from London to attend the ceremonies. I actually wasn't going to bother turning up to receive the certificate, but Lily said that with my folks travelling all that way it was foolish to have a rebellious attitude. So I rented the graduation gown and mortarboard and took my place amongst the thousands in the auditorium. When my name was called, I took the stage to receive my certificate. The chancellor (who had no idea who I was) flippantly said "You made it" as he shook my hand. He most probably said that to all the graduating students, but it resonated with me as if he was familiar with my unusual journey. I had a bachelor of arts degree. My parents were proud. Lily and I were proud. But it really could just as easily have been a bachelor of farts. It was like climbing a mountain. You journey all that way to get to the top, pleased for the conquest, but once there it's all over. You have to just go back down. An English degree was basically worthless. I needed a job, but it was one of the worst economic periods of the modern era.

# CHAPTER 23

# New World Order

As the high-flying 1970s gave way to the reality of the 1980s, a recession smacked society to the ground. In Canada, unemployment grew steadily right through to 1982, peaking at 12.9 percent — a level that had not been matched since the 1930s. Inflation was spiralling out of control — over 10 percent in Canada, and peaking at over 14 percent in the United States in April 1980. There was a crisis in Iran. Over sixty Americans working at the embassy had been taken hostage. The majority of them would be held for 444 days. Oil prices skyrocketed to over thirty-five dollars a barrel (over one hundred dollars in today's money). The automobile industry was rocked. The environmental scandal at Niagara Falls' Love Canal highlighted the past arrogance of big industry. Thousands of barrels of toxic waste had been dumped into the water over the years, causing extreme health problems for the residents. It was just one example, albeit extreme, illustrating that poisons were in our own backyards. The potential for nuclear catastrophe was headlined by the March 1979 disaster at Three Mile Island, when a major nuclear meltdown occurred. Economically, the Western world looked for a new path. This would be the era of Margaret Thatcher and Ronald Reagan and unbridled free enterprise.

In Vancouver, things were bleak. The city was still relatively undiscovered. It was more deserted warehouses than high-priced condos. The Whistler Blackcomb ski resort, north of the city (destined to be one of the best in the world), was only just starting to be developed. And then on May 18, 1980, the volcano Mount St. Helens in Washington State, five hundred kilometres south of Vancouver, exploded, killing over fifty people. The ash, carried north by the wind, fell like grey snow on the cars, gardens, and houses in the city. It was an ominous sign.

Things were even bad for Fulham FC. They were relegated once again to Division Three after winning only eleven of forty-two matches that 1979 to 1980 season.

Thinking I could turn my English degree into something useful, I saw a newspaper want ad from a well-known Toronto publishing company for campus representatives to oversee their line of educational books. It wasn't as flimsy as the Australian door-to-door encyclopedia salesperson job, but I did find the connection amusing. I applied, and after a series of interviews I was offered the job. But there was a catch. Given the harsh economic times, the company had closed its West Coast offices and laid off all its support staff. In order to qualify for the job, I had to use my home address as the office address, and even my home phone was to be the contact number. (That was a mistake.) In return, I was given a small wage and a splendid new car, and my work schedule was my own. I took the job.

I was flown to Toronto to meet my new bosses, see the big office, and take part in five days of indoctrination. It was my first corporate business trip. I had made it to the big city. The company accommodated me in the Carlton Hotel, next to the famed hockey arena Maple Leaf Gardens. It was all very exciting. At the company headquarters, they gave me a lesson in how to sell the books and how to keep track of and fill in my expense sheets, and I was presented with stylish business cards printed with not only my name but also my home address and phone number. I met the other new recruits who had been hired for the other parts of Canada. Like me, they were recent university grads and thrilled to be gainfully employed in tough times. I felt important, but I was beginning to have feelings of regret. In the morning, I had my breakfast in the hotel restaurant. Almost every seat at every table was taken with hotel guests. But these were not casual tourists. Every one of them was a salesperson. They were almost all men, in the same grey suit, with the same haircut, with black briefcases placed on the floor by their feet, with day planners open on the table. It was like a scene out of a sci-fi movie. They drank their coffee and conversed about closed deals and commissions. I realized I was now one of them.

The company organized a dinner at a posh Toronto restaurant. It wasn't just to welcome and impress the new hires but also to welcome employees of a famed British publishing house that the Canadian company had just acquired. The acquisition added not only a famous brand but also prestige to the Canadian upstart, plus a vast array of respected books and authors. This was cause for celebration. There were over twenty people seated at the extra-long restaurant table, from senior executives to new recruits. I was sitting next to one of my British counterparts, a young man who had never been to Canada. Atlantic lobster was ordered for everybody. When the red-shelled, oversized creatures were placed in front of each diner, a small bowl of relatively clear liquid was added alongside. For fun, plastic bibs with cartoon lobster creatures were also handed out in case eating the shellfish was too messy. We all tucked into our splendid meal. The English chap next to me cracked open his meal with his hands, consumed the white meat, and then dunked his sticky fingers in what he thought was the finger bowl beside his plate. It wasn't water. It was melted butter. He lifted his hands out and held them high. The butter started to run down his hands and arms. The party at the table looked at him in partial bemusement, with "My God, how could you?" faces. The waiter ran over with a towel and helped the young man clean his hands and arms. Full of embarrassment, he then excused himself to wash his hands. He laughed it off in a gentle way. But it could have been me. I had never had lobster before either.

After dinner we were all invited back to one of the hotel rooms in the Carlton for drinks and casual conversation. Jokes, stories of outlandish sales adventures, and other war exploits were exchanged among all who were gathered together in those close quarters. The man who had hired me then remembered that I had mentioned in the original interview that I wrote poetry. Could I entertain the troops with some of my work? There were one or two poems that I remembered by heart, and so I proudly spoke aloud my punk- and new-wave-infused creations. That was about as smart a thing as dipping my hands in melted butter. It got just about the same reaction.

Back in Vancouver in my new position of WCC (West Coast Campus) rep, the impressive catalogue of books began to arrive in boxes at our basement door. There were so many that they quickly began to rival the record collection in terms of space. They ranged from the basic English 100 collection of poetry and short stories to esoteric philosophy books aimed at fourth-year students. Also, unfortunately, the home phone rang with callers looking for the West Coast office of the publishing company. It became so frustrating that we did not answer the phone at all and let it go to the answering machine.

With my blemish-free, white embossed business card in hand, my job was to introduce myself to the professors who taught the various courses, present them with the book, give them the pitch as to how this particular book was more advanced than the text that they were already recommending as part of the curriculum, and then hope that the book was assigned as a core reading material for the course. It turned out to be another exercise in economic learning.

In its own way, the book industry paralleled the music industry. I had to find a hit, the lowest common denominator. The emphasis was on books used in the big first-year courses: English, psychology, and economics. The reason? Pure numbers. There were hundreds of students signed up for those courses, so if a professor made a particular text the handbook of that course, sales would not only spike but also likely be entrenched for many years after. I, of course, worked the hardest on those books that I thought were wonderful and whose ideas inspired me. They were aimed at courses that usually had only about ten students enrolled. Even if the book was assigned to a course, sales were meager. Forget creativity and think of the commission, I was told.

The company decided that one of the senior reps from the American branch should come up from Seattle to spend a day with me. My Toronto bosses told me that this guy was a legend. His sales record was one of the best in the company. He had received the Salesperson of the Year accolade a number of times. I could learn a lot from him, they said. After exchanging phone calls with the gentleman in question, he told me he was driving up mid-week. I arranged to meet him at the student union building on the UBC campus; at least I knew my way around that campus, as well as some of the professors.

Joe was a nice man. Twice my age, about fifty-five. Large fellow. Smoked a lot. Had the gift of the gab and knew the publishing catalogue back to front. He also was excited about the acquisition of the British company. It gave him more things to sell. We got along well. He gave me a crucial piece of advice. Instead of visiting all the professors who, say, taught the English 100 course and leaving each one a copy of the book in question, find the one professor who was in charge of assigning the texts and just leave a single copy. "Time management," he said. He also advised me to "Read the notice boards — find out who is conducting special seminars. Get them the specialized texts." Joe was good at his job. After spending the morning touring the campus offices, introducing ourselves to various professors, Joe wanted to go for lunch. I recommended a few places, including the cafeteria in the student union building. They had excellent cinnamon buns. Oh no, he said, he wanted to go to a pub. Not just any pub, but one with strippers. He had heard about the famous Vancouver strip scene! He wanted to leave his car in the campus parking lot, so I drove my new, stylish company car.

After he had had a couple of pints, and more than a few dances from Vancouver's finest "ballet" stars, Joe suggested we go back to my basement apartment so that he could see how the files and books were set up. Once there, he wanted nothing more to do with work. He had heard I had a background as a DJ and wondered whether I could play him some tunes. I choose an album by a new English band called Dire Straits. Joe made himself comfortable on the couch and then proceeded to pull out a chunk of brown hash and a pipe as casually as if he had pulled out the company's new English dictionary from his oversized publishing bag.

"Got this before I left. See those black speckles?" He held up the hash between two fingers so that I could admire its texture. "That's opium."

Holy cow! Was I going to have the number one salesman in the west sprawled out on the floor of my basement apartment like some casualty from *Apocalypse Now*? He broke off a small chunk and crushed it between his fingers, and the crumbs fell into the bowl of the pipe. He struck a match and inhaled, holding the smoke in for a few seconds, and then exhaled, filling the air with a thick, sweet cloud. With that familiar collapsed-lung look, he offered some to me. I declined. The idea of opium put me off. While "Sultans of Swing" played, Joe proceeded to give me the benefit of his years of wisdom, representing some of the greatest writers and thinkers of our time. "And if you sell a lot of books, you can have a great life," he told me. "Man, great tune," he added. Joe was enjoying himself.

After a couple of hours of his extraordinary company, and with twilight approaching, Joe said it was time for him to return to Seattle. He needed me to drive him back out to his car at the UBC parking lot. He assured me he was okay to drive.

There is not one UBC parking lot, but many. And they are huge. They are categorized by letter (*A*, *B*, *C*, and so on) for easy remembrance. Forget your letter, and you can forget your car. Such was the case with Joe. He had only a vague idea of the location. We spent about an hour driving from parking lot to parking lot until we finally found his vehicle. I was glad of that, because it allowed him to come back down to earth. After saying our overly friendly goodbyes, he headed south for Seattle and reality. Such was my afternoon with the top salesman in the company.

My territory for the company included not only British Columbia, but Alberta and Saskatchewan. After visiting all the universities and colleges around Vancouver, I made plans to fly to Edmonton to work the University of Alberta. It was winter, so I had to make allowances for the weather. Heavy boots and parka were needed if I was going to hoof it around the sprawling campus. Just before I left, my boss called me from Toronto with sad news. One of the other young reps who had been hired at the same time as me had been killed while driving on the treacherous 401 highway outside of Toronto. I was sad. I didn't know him well, having spent no more than a couple of hours with him over beers at the bar during our original indoctrination period, but somehow his death represented the pointlessness of the whole thing. Trying to get ahead in life and being killed on the job. He was driving his new company car.

My mood was not great when I checked into a cheap motel on Edmonton's Whyte Avenue. Dirty snow and ice packed the city tight. Bland meals in the motel restaurant were more appealing than the frozen wind that tortured the streets. Back in my room, I was racked out on the bed watching bad TV. I plotted my strategy for my assault on campus and zeroed in on the company's number one priority — a compendium of short stories, essays, and poems aimed at the lucrative English 100 course. The campus directory listed numerous professors and teaching assistants who taught the course. I cross-referenced it with a map of the offices, so I knew where to go. I also had to find the senior professor to give them the big spiel and offer as many of the fine books in the company catalogue as necessary to help sweeten the pitch.

After spending several hours walking through the corridors, knocking on doors, glad-handing, and giving my sales pitch and business card, I located the office of one of the senior English professors. His name had an unusual spelling, and I was unsure of how to pronounce it. I knocked on his door, and I heard the word "enter" come from the other side. I walked into a cluttered office, filled with shelves weighed down with books and a busy desk covered in papers. I introduced myself as the new rep from the company as we shook hands. I also asked if I had pronounced his name correctly. He looked at me bewildered and possibly insulted. I continued to talk about how great this new collection of short stories and poems was, and how it might be perfect for his course. He listened patiently without interrupting. When I finished talking, he made no comment about the book I was offering but mentioned the news item about the company I worked for acquiring the storied British publishing company.

"So you are the rep for not only the Canadian company, but for the books that come out under this British group as well?" he asked me.

"Well, yes," I said.

"So how are my books doing?"

"Pardon me?"

"Yes, my novels," he said, and with that he turned around and proceeded to pull out half a dozen paperback novels from the shelf from behind his desk. "You are, in theory, my rep as well. My books are published by the British company."

"Oh," I said. As it turns out, this gentleman was one of the most well-respected authors in western Canada. Ouch. All I could do was plead my innocence as the new man on the job. "But why don't I call the Toronto head office to find out the status of your work? Can I use your phone?" I asked.

"Go ahead."

I dialed the 1-800 number and got through to my boss. He explained the situation to the professor in question. I was a new guy, still learning the ropes, the acquisition of the British company was recent, and they didn't want to burden me with too much information. I left the office embarrassed. I never forgot the fact that I had done a disservice to, as it turns out, one of western Canada's most famous authors. (Twenty-five years later, when I was the host and producer for BookTV, the writer in question won a prestigious award for his body of work. I was tasked with creating a television profile of the author. I spared no expense by way of compensating for that slight so many years before.)

Shortly after my return to Vancouver, I wrote a letter to the company resigning my position. I had tried to go straight. I had tried a real job. And I had hated it. My boss telephoned a couple of days later to say he understood my decision. He also mentioned that it came as no surprise to the head office executives. I asked why, and he said that after the corporate get-together in the Carlton Hotel a memo had been circulated stating that I would most probably quit the position because I wrote poetry! Even to this day, that observation strikes me as interesting, as if it somehow summed up the tension between the "real" economic world and the world of the imagination.

I returned to my records and my role as a DJ. It was at this time that I heard one particular song: Joy Division's "Love Will Tear Us Apart." I loved it. It was the sound of a new direction. A new world. A new wave. I felt empowered. Eventually new wave became the music of the moment, and I found myself spinning tunes at Vancouver's notorious Luv-A-Fair club, arguably one of the most influential new music clubs in North America at the time. It was dark, loud, and musically brilliant, and I found myself in the middle of a cultural explosion, which was very exciting. But the joy of "Good Times" had been obliterated by politics, evolution, and the reality of a new world. The first cases of AIDS began to appear in the spring of 1980. The innocent, carefree nights were over. It was the love I lost. It was time we all lost as we danced the night away. Disco didn't die; just the name did. Dance music mutated into various forms as it entered the 1980s: synth-pop, house, techno. It found a new path. Just like I did. So did the whole world.

I eventually became manager of one of Canada's pioneer electronic bands, Images in Vogue, and that, in turn, led me to being hired by MuchMusic television in Toronto as a VJ and producer. I was on the front lines of rock 'n' roll, and I travelled the world reporting on its industry. But that's another story.

# Acknowledgements

A special thanks to Shannon Whibbs who offered me the Dundurn deal; to Kathryn Lane for editorial guidance; and to Andrea Douglas for the edit suggestions. A shout out to Michael Holmes at ECW Press who initially gave me wonderful words of encouragement.

This book, and this colourful life, would not be possible without the love, support, and belief of my parents Gwen and Gerry Champniss. Love you. Thanks for everything. To my siblings Waynne, Basil, Alex, and Karimah (and their partners), thanks for being there. Waynne, wherever you are, sorry you cannot be here to celebrate this book's publication. You helped make it happen. Cheers!

To those who travelled with me down this road, thank you for the company and the adventures: Mick Sherlock, Barry Hubert, Jerry Don Carolis, Larry Lawlis, Doug Moore, the Calgary crowd (Terry Lee Walker, Terry Millhouse, Mary Romano, Bernice Bolin, and many more), and the Vancouver disco crowd. Thanks to Alice Delaney-Walker for encouragement all those student years ago, the late Warren Tallman, and George McWhirter. And a special thank-you to the residents of Arviat when it was known as Eskimo Point. What an amazing time.

For friendship, help, and encouragement in more recent times: Tony Dean, Marie Boutilier, and Bill Bobek. Thank you.

And, of course, Lily.

Keep on dancing.